Natural
HOME REMEDIES

Natural
HOME REMEDIES

*Safe, effective and traditional
treatments for common ailments*

MARK EVANS B PHIL., FNIMH

Sebastian Kelly

This edition published by
Sebastian Kelly
2 Rectory Road
Oxford OX4 1BW

Produced by
Anness Publishing Limited
Hermes House, 88-89 Blackfriars Road
London SE1 8HA

ISBN 1-84081-008-4

A CIP catalogue record for this book
is available from the British Library

Publisher: Joanna Lorenz
Editorial Manager: Helen Sudell
Designer: Nigel Partridge
Photographer: Lucy Mason

Printed in Singapore by Star Standard Industries Pte. Ltd.

© 1996 Anness Publishing Limited
Updated © 1998
1 3 5 7 9 10 8 6 4 2

IMPORTANT NOTICE
The advice given in this book is appropriate in most cases. However, it
cannot take into account specific individuals' reactions. Neither the author
nor the publishers can accept any responsibility for claims arising from the
inappropriate use of any remedy or healing treatment. For further advice,
and before beginning any treatment suggested herein, read page 121 for
information pertaining to certain conditions and herb restrictions.

CONTENTS

INTRODUCTION

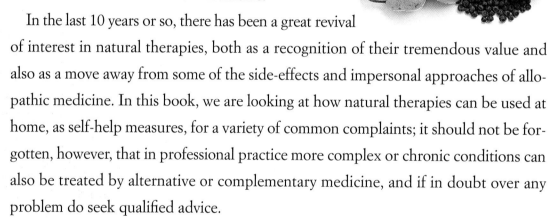

Health is, or should be, the most natural state of being. The origins of the word are linked with those of wholeness and healing, and it is that complete sense of harmony, of being whole, that brings true health. This is also the ultimate aim of the natural healing systems, those that adopt a holistic view rather than the reductionist perspective that is evident in much of conventional modern medicine.

In the last 10 years or so, there has been a great revival of interest in natural therapies, both as a recognition of their tremendous value and also as a move away from some of the side-effects and impersonal approaches of allopathic medicine. In this book, we are looking at how natural therapies can be used at home, as self-help measures, for a variety of common complaints; it should not be forgotten, however, that in professional practice more complex or chronic conditions can also be treated by alternative or complementary medicine, and if in doubt over any problem do seek qualified advice.

Many traditions of natural medicine extend back over several centuries, with an impressive accumulation of practical knowledge. For this book we have focused on four main therapies, which not only have such an established tradition but also have good standards of training, clinical research data and widespread acceptance. They are aromatherapy, herbalism, homeopathy and naturopathy.

ABOVE: Fresh fruit is an excellent natural source of vitamins.

OPPOSITE: Herbs can be grown successfully in ordinary garden flower beds, giving off wonderful scents as well as providing a useful source of herbal medicines.

AROMATHERAPY

The use of pure essential oils from plants dates back many centuries, and the history of aromatherapy is in many ways part of the history of herbal medicine as a whole. The Arabic countries are credited with first discovering the process of distillation of oils, around a thousand years ago, and since then their use has spread both eastwards through the Indian sub-continent and westwards into Europe. Much modern research has taken place, for example, in France, ranging from perfumery applications to medicinal uses as powerful anti-infective agents.

Essential oils are highly concentrated substances – pure oil of Rose, for instance, may require 5,000 roses to make just 5 ml (1 tsp) of oil! For this reason they should be treated with respect and used sparingly – small is definitely better (and cheaper). In large doses many essential oils can become somewhat irritating to the skin, and a few are quite toxic if not used correctly. See general warning on page 121.

Since a large part of their effect on our moods and emotional states occurs through our sense of smell, it is important not to use any individual oil for too long, as they become tolerated and less useful. As a general rule, do not use an oil on a daily basis for more than 10 days. Similarly, do not inhale

Essential oils are very concentrated: add a drop at a time and only use the amounts suggested.

or mix too many oils together at one time; the olfactory centre in the brain becomes confused and an excess of essences can cause headaches or even nausea. Three or at the most four oils should be the maximum; two may be better.

A common way to use essential oils for self-treatment is in the bath. Place 6 drops on the surface of the bath water just before entering. The drops quickly form a thin film over the surface which adheres to the skin and is partially absorbed, helped by the warmth of the water. For oils such as Peppermint, which can make the skin tingle if used in large amounts, just add 3-4 drops, whereas with a mild and generally very safe oil such as Lavender, 10 drops can be used. If using a blend, the above suggestions represent the total number of drops to use in the bath. For compresses, use a maximum of 5 drops in a small bowl of hot or cold water as directed in this book (see page 15).

Another important method for using oils is diluted into a base vegetable oil and applied to the skin in massage. For home use a general dilution rate should be 1 per cent; since essential oils are usually sold in dropper bottles, this means a maximum of 20 drops per 100 ml (4 fl oz/½ cup) of base oil. Different cultures over the centuries have favoured various vegetable oils for massage, mostly dependent on local availability. Probably the most versatile oil is that of Sweet Almond; it is absorbed well into the skin and helps to nourish the skin, too. Other good base oils are Grapeseed, Sunflower and Safflower; the lightest oil of all is Coconut, but it may become solid at cool temperatures.

Keep aromatherapy oils in well-stoppered bottles, out of the sun, when not in use.

HERBALISM

Herbal medicine is the most widespread of all forms of medicine across the world, both historically and even today. At some time all cultures have used herbalism as the main system of treatment; its origins are essentially the origins of mankind itself. Probably the earliest herbal tradition comes from India. Medical knowledge from there spread into China on the one hand and into the Middle East on the other. The philosophy underlying Ancient Egyptian, and later Graeco-Roman, medicine has many similarities with both the old Ayur-Vedic system from northern India and traditional Chinese medicine.

Modern Western herbal medicine stems from the knowledge of the Greeks, with a strong input from the Native American tradition too. Increasingly, research being carried out today often confirms centuries-old empirical knowledge. Around 80 per cent of the world's population still relies on herbal medicine for their health needs, and even within conventional Western medicine up to 20 per cent of drugs are derived from plants in one way or another.

Herbs are almost certainly the most popular method of self-help in minor complaints, and introduce people to natural medicine. Throughout this book you will find references to how to take herbs internally; the easiest method is to make a tea, using a rough rule of 5 ml (1 tsp) per person plus the same for the teapot (many of the most popular herbs are available in tea bags, simply use one of these). If using fresh herbs, for example Lemon Balm *(Melissa officinalis)* you can use double the above amounts.

For stronger, more medicinal brews, you need to make either an infusion or a decoction (see page 12). For either an infusion or a decoction, the standard dose is 100-150 ml (4-5 fl oz/½-⅔ cup) – approximately a medium-sized teacupful – three times a day.

These infusions and decoctions can also be used to make a compress or poultice (see page 15). Once again, if using fresh herbs you can use more, perhaps 50 per cent more of each herb.

Many of the herbs found in gardens today have been used by herbalists for over two thousand years.

HOMEOPATHY

As a full system of medicine, homeopathy is much more recent in its development. It owes its modern origins to Samuel Hahnemann, a German physician, who formulated homeopathic theories in the late eighteenth century, although the principles were almost certainly known for hundreds of years before. Essentially, symptoms are seen not as negative effects of illness but as the attempts of the person to resist disease. Hahnemann tested a treatment for malaria on himself by taking many doses of quinine; after some time he induced malarial-like symptoms, and came to the conclusion that quinine worked precisely because it created these reactions in a healthy person; it mimicked and supported our own healing responses.

This led to the principle of "like curing like", and hundreds of homeopathic remedies have since been tested by giving them to healthy people and recording the responses. These "remedy pictures" are then applied to see which one fits the symptoms of an ill person. The other major point of difference between homeopathic and conventional medicine is that when a remedy has been identified as being appropriate to encourage the individual's self-healing mechanisms, it is then prescribed in minute amounts. Hahnemann had found that by diluting his remedies in a special way he was able to get a quicker effect, and he understood these dilutions to work on a more subtle level than simply obtaining a physical reaction.

One of the common scales for measuring the dilutions is the centesimal scale – that is, diluting the remedy in the ratio of 1:100. For a liquid this means one part of the remedy is mixed with 99 parts of a diluent, usually either alcohol or water. This is called a 1c dilution; this is then shaken in a special way, or succussed, and one part of this is added to 99 parts of the diluent to make a 2c dilution, and so on. As you can see, levels of extreme dilution are quickly reached, and so the remedy cannot be said to be acting physically in a conventional way, and indeed an important part of the "remedy picture" is the emotional reactions that are produced. The personality of the patient is a significant factor in choosing a remedy. Paradoxically, the more dilute the remedy, the more effectively it works.

A homeopathic practitioner may well use a very diluted remedy, to address an imbalance in our basic constitution, if there is a very clear picture that matches the individual.

For self-help treatment choose either the 6c or 30c potencies. For mild problems try taking the 6c dilution (normally remedies are available as tablets or pills, with directions for taking them with the container they come in) 3 times a day for up to 5 days. In more acute conditions, take a 30c dilution in the same way.

In short-term, really acute conditions you can take up to 6 doses of either potency at 3-hourly intervals. Continuing to take the remedies for longer, however, may result in an aggravation of symptoms, as you "prove" the remedy in the same way that Hahnemann did. If in any doubt, and in any case if there is no response within this time, always see a professional homeopath.

ACONITE
(Aconitum napellus)

Homeopathic remedies are made from a number of substances, plant, animal or mineral, and diluted in a special manner.

NATUROPATHY

In many respects, naturopathy is really common sense applied to health. The basic principle is that we have tremendous innate healing abilities, and our systems will always attempt to overcome an illness and restore balance. In naturopathy, these attempts are encouraged by utilizing such natural factors as diet, exercise and relaxation, fresh air and the use of water (hydrotherapy). The general thrust of treatment is really to shift responsibility for health back to ourselves as far as possible, and equally to advocate prevention rather than cure.

Increasingly nowadays, ill-health is recognized as arising from environmental factors such as pollution, so an individual can only do so much to keep healthy, and wider measures may well need to be campaigned for. Nevertheless, a lot can be done through self-help action. While fresh, unprocessed foods are the main form of dietary treatment, there are times when this needs to be supplemented in order to raise vitality to a level where self-healing can take place, and so throughout the book there are some suggestions for supplements under different headings.

Exercise is a major form of self-help, obviously within limits of individual comfort. Both posture and correct breathing are an integral part of this, as effort without correct breathing can lead to strain. It is important to ensure that adequate rest or relaxation is taken too (easier to say than do in today's busy world!), and naturopaths would certainly give advice on these areas as part of the treatment.

The application of water by various methods, or hydrotherapy treatment, is another very useful part of naturopathy. The concept of using hot or cold water dates back at least to the Ancient Greeks, and is seen around the world in other old cultures, for example, that of Native Americans. Hydrotherapy treatment had a major revival in

The importance of regular exercise to keep our whole body fit, active and healthy is now well-recognized.

Europe in the nineteenth century, with the Bavarian monk Sebastian Kneipp the most influential figure. To this day, there are many Kneipp centres in Germany, Austria and Switzerland, which still prove very popular with patients. There are also around 120 different hydrotherapy treatments available in German health spas.

One of the simplest methods is to use a compress, or fomentation, made by wringing out a small towel in water and placing over the required area (see page 15). By alternating hot and cold compresses, – normally about 3-5 minutes if hot and up to 1 minute if cold – the local circulation can be strongly stimulated. For people who are considerably overweight it is often better just to use a cool compress, as this is less taxing on the heart. A shower can be used to similar effect by changing the temperature, or cool splashes of water after a warm bath may be used. A specific form of treatment in hydrotherapy clinics is the use of sitz baths, a kind of hip bath, which works on the pelvic and abdominal areas, by sitting firstly in a hot bath then transferring to a cold one for a short time, as indicated above.

As well as these approaches to health and healing, natural therapies range from those that work mainly via the body, such as massage, osteopathy, chiropractic and physiotherapy, through those that deal with energy balance, such as acupuncture, reflexology and shiatsu, to those that approach from the mental or emotional level, such as hypnotherapy, psychotherapy and group work. Each has its own strengths and weaknesses, and each attempts to help to restore balance from its own perspective. Some of them are not so easily applied for self-help, but it is useful to know that if you are unable to sort out your health problems on your own, then there is a wide choice of professional treatments that may help.

MAKING AN INFUSION

An infusion is made by pouring boiling water over an amount of the herb, to extract the properties. It is suitable for leaves and flowers, whose parts are easily extracted.

1 Place the herb in a teapot with a close-fitting lid. Pour in boiling water. Leave to infuse for up to 10 minutes.

2 Strain through a sieve or strainer into a cup. Store the remainder in a jug, preferably in the fridge.

STANDARD QUANTITIES
25 g (1 oz) dried herb or 50 g (2 oz) fresh herb to 500 ml (16 fl oz/2 cups) boiling water.

STANDARD DOSES
One teacup (approximately 150 ml (5 fl oz/⅔ cup)) 3 times a day.

Infusions and decoctions should be stored in tightly-stoppered vessels ideally, and will last for about 3 days in the fridge.

MAKING A DECOCTION

A decoction involves simmering the herb in water to extract its properties, and is suitable for roots or woody parts that do not easily yield their ingredients in a simple infusion. If combining two plants, where one is a root, say Dandelion (*Taraxacum officinale*), and the other a flower, say Chamomile (*Chamomilla recutita*), use the strained decoction of the former for pouring on to the latter to make the infusion.

1 Place the herb in a saucepan and pour on cold water. Bring to the boil and simmer, until the liquid is reduced by a third.

2 Strain through a sieve into a jug, and store in a fridge. It will keep for up to three days.

STANDARD QUANTITIES
25 g (1 oz) dried herb or 50 g (2 oz) fresh herb to 750 ml (1¼ pt/3⅔ cups) water, reduced to 500 ml (16 fl oz/2 cups) after simmering.

STANDARD DOSES
One teacup (150 ml (5 fl oz/⅔ cup)) 3 times a day.

MAKING A HOT OIL INFUSION

Herbs can be infused in oil, to make an extract for use in massage, or in making creams and ointments. Infused oils may keep for a few months, but will be stronger made in small batches for more immediate use. Hot infused oils may be made from herbs such as Comfrey (*Symphytum officinale*), while flowers such as Marigold (*Calendula officinalis*) or St John's Wort (*Hypericum perforatum*) are better as cold infused oils. Any light oil, such as Sunflower, Safflower or Sweet Almond oil, is a suitable medium to use.

MAKING A COLD OIL INFUSION

Some plants contain important medicinal oils which are highly volatile, i.e. they escape with heat, and a cold oil infusion retains their properties much more successfully.

1 Place the herb and oil in a glass bowl, over a saucepan of simmering water, and heat gently for a couple of hours.

2 Pour through a jelly bag into a clean jug.

3 Squeeze out as much oil as possible through the bag (wear gloves as the oil is hot), to get a really strong extract.

4 Pour into clean, dark bottles. Seal and store. Keep in a cool place and use within 3 months of making.

1 Pack a large jar with the herb and cover with oil. Seal and leave in a sunny spot for 2 weeks.

2 Pour slowly through a jelly bag into a clean jug, allowing time for the oil to filter through the fabric.

3 Squeeze out as much oil as possible through the bag. To make the infused oil even stronger, repeat steps 1, 2 and 3 with the same oil and new amounts of the herb.

4 Pour into clean, dark bottles. Seal and store. Preferably, use small bottles as when opened the oil starts to deteriorate.

STANDARD QUANTITIES
250 g (9 oz) dried herb or 500 g (1¼ lb) fresh herb to 500 ml (16 fl oz/2 cups) pure vegetable oil.

STANDARD QUANTITIES
250 g (9 oz) dried herb or 500 g (1¼ lb) fresh herb to 500 ml (16 fl oz/2 cups) pure vegetable oil.

MAKING A TINCTURE

Many herbs contain active ingredients which are not easily extracted by water, or are destroyed by heat, and a tincture solves these problems as well as preserving the extract. A tincture is an extract of a herb in a mixture of alcohol and water, normally 25 per cent alcohol strength. This is one of the most concentrated extracts from a herb, and the alcohol preserves the medicine for 2 years or more. The alcohol used commercially is ethyl alcohol, but a spirit such as brandy or vodka can be used for home tinctures. Do not use industrial alcohol, isopropyl alcohol or methylated spirits, as they are all poisonous.

Because a tincture is such a concentrated extract, only use where recommended, and for short periods of time. Do not be tempted to increase the dosage.

1 Put the herb into a large jar and pour on the alcohol/water mixture. Seal the jar and store in a cool place for two weeks. Shake the jar occasionally.

2 Pour mixture through a jelly bag into a clean jug.

BUCHU (*Barosma betulina*)

CAUTION

If in any doubt about using a tincture, seek professional advice, or stick to the other methods described in this book. Do not give tinctures to children, unless advised, and remember to keep all medicines out of the reach of small children.

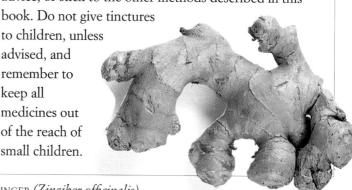

GINGER (*Zingiber officinalis*)

3 Squeeze out the tincture from the bag. Ideally, use a wine press and press the mixture into a clean jug.

4 Pour the strained liquid into clean, dark bottles. Seal and store. Keep in a cool dry place and label.

STANDARD QUANTITIES

200 g (7 oz) dried herb or 40 g (1½ oz) fresh herb to 1 litre (1¾ pt/4 cups) 25 per cent alcohol/water mix (e.g. if using 40 per cent vodka or brandy, add 375 ml (13 fl oz/1½ cups) water to 600 ml (1 pt/2½ cups) spirit to make a 25 per cent strength).

STANDARD DOSES

Up to 5 ml (1 tsp), three times a day. These may be taken diluted in a little water. For concentrated herbs such as Ginger (*Zingiber officinalis*), take up to 10 drops, 3 times a day. Preferably take these with water.

WARM AND COLD COMPRESSES

A compress is a way of applying herbal extracts directly to the skin, to reduce the inflammation or promote healing. Usually, an infusion or decoction of the herb is prepared for use in the compress, or simply hot or cold water can be used.

1 Soak a clean cloth or flannel in a hot infusion or hot water.

2 Place on the affected area and hold firmly in place – use a towel or bandage to tie in place if kept on for long. The same procedure applies for cold compresses.

*Marigold (*Calendula officinalis) *is very soothing for bites and stings.*

POULTICE

A poultice acts in a similar way to a compress, but the herb itself is used, rather than just a liquid extract. Normally poultices are applied hot, and it may be useful to apply a little oil to the skin first, to stop the herb from sticking.

1 Chop up the fresh herb if it is too large, and place sufficient herbs to cover the affected area into a saucepan. Add a little water and simmer for a couple of minutes.

2 Squeeze out any excess moisture and place on the affected area. Cover with a bandage or cotton strips to hold in place.

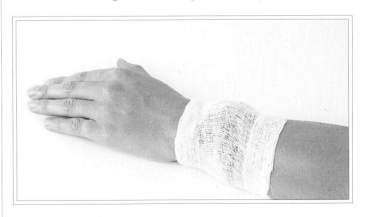

3 Keep in place for 3-4 hours, replacing every hour with a fresh, hot poultice if necessary.

MAKING AN OINTMENT

An ointment contains oils or fats, but not water, and is useful to form a protective layer over the skin. Petroleum jelly or paraffin wax may be used, but a wonderful natural method is to use vegetable oil, such as Sweet Almond or Sunflower, with beeswax. This is also very easy to make at home.

MAKING A CREAM

Making an organic cream is very similar to making an ointment, again using beeswax.

1 Place beeswax and oil in a glass bowl in a saucepan of water (see left). Bring water to the boil and simmer until the wax has melted. Place water in another glass bowl, over a saucepan of simmering water. Remove both glass bowls from the heat.

1 Place the beeswax and oil in a glass bowl over a saucepan of water. Bring the water to the boil and simmer until the wax has melted into the oil. Remove from the heat.

2 Add water to the melted wax/oil mixture, drop by drop, stirring all the time until the cream thickens and cools.

3 At this stage essential oils may be added, as recommended, and gently stirred into the cream.

2 Stir continually as the oil/wax mixture cools and stiffens; essential oils may be added at this stage, as recommended, and stirred into the mixture.

3 Pour or spoon into small, clean ointment jars, seal and store. This may keep for a few months under good conditions, but should be made in small amounts as needed.

4 Pour or spoon into small, clean ointment jars, seal and store. Make small amounts as required. This cream may keep for a few months under good conditions.

STANDARD QUANTITIES
25 g (1 oz) beeswax to 100 ml (4 fl oz/½ cup) vegetable oil.
If adding essential oils, use 20-30 drops for this amount, but only 10 drops if skin is very sensitive.

STANDARD QUANTITIES
25 g (1 oz) beeswax, 25 ml (1½ tbsp) water and 100 ml (4 fl oz/½ cup) vegetable oil. If adding essential oils, use 20-30 drops at the most for this amount of cream.

MIXING ESSENTIAL OILS FOR MASSAGE

When essential oils are used for aromatherapy massage, different oils are combined to increase their therapeutic effect. Light vegetable oils such as Sweet Almond, Grapeseed or Sunflower are the best oils to begin with. For home use the general dilution rate should be 1 per cent (i.e. a maximum of 20 drops per 100 ml (4 fl oz/½ cup) of base oil). Once you have mixed your oils, store in a cool, dark place and use them immediately, as they are perishable.

2 Gently pour the vegetable oil into your blending bowl.

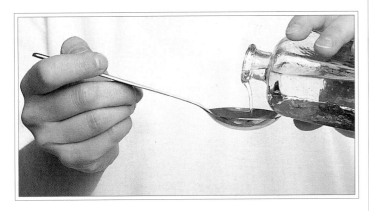

1 Before you begin, wash and dry your hands and make sure that all your utensils are clean and dry. Have your essential oils at the ready, but leave the lids on the bottles until they are required. Carefully measure out approximately 10 ml (2 tsp) of your chosen vegetable oil.

CAUTION

The essential oil recommendations in this book are extremely safe in the amounts given. If someone has very sensitive skin or lots of allergies then try massaging with just one drop of essential oil per 20 ml (4 tsp) of base oil at first to test for any signs of reaction (rare). If the person is pregnant or may be pregnant, stick to the oils and doses suggested in the chapter on reproduction. If in any doubt, seek medical advice.

3 Add the essential oil, one drop at a time. Mix gently with a clean, dry cocktail stick or toothpick, to blend.

THE NERVOUS SYSTEM

One of the main principles of natural medicine is the holistic approach, taking into account the physical, mental, emotional and indeed spiritual well-being of the person when assessing health; this is most obviously apparent when looking at nervous disorders. Physical symptoms, such as headaches or insomnia, and emotional ones, such as depression, mental strains and stresses, can all weave together to create disease, or simply *dis-ease* – a lack of harmony.

When trying to treat these problems, therefore, it is essential to look at all the reasons for the disorder. One of the first things to do is apply some common sense: is your headache due to an excess of alcohol last night, does your anxiety stem from tomorrow's interview, or your insomnia follow three cups of coffee in the evening? Finding the cause may not solve your immediate problem, but may help you to take preventive steps. In many cases of course, the causes are not so obvious and for persistent or recurring problems professional help should be sought.

Apart from the therapies described in this book, there are many sources of help for nerve-related conditions – since stress is a major factor in much ill-health nowadays, most forms of alternative medicine look at this aspect in their approaches. These might range from counselling and hypnotherapy through to acupuncture and cranial osteopathy. Equally importantly, these should all help to empower *you* to help yourself more effectively, which is the key aim of this book.

ABOVE: Taking time to relax and unwind is important for the overall well-being of our nervous system.

ANXIETY

There are many situations where some level of anxiety is perfectly normal, and a natural response to a stressful situation. It only becomes a problem when the degree of anxiety is out of proportion to the problem, or indeed when there is no objective, external reason for it. Symptoms might include constant feelings of tension, sweating, palpitations, hyper-ventilating and lack of sleep.

ROSE *(Rosa)*

AROMATHERAPY

There are several oils which have a relaxing, calming effect on the nervous system; probably the nicest way to use them is in the bath (see page 17), where the warm water aids relaxation and helps the oils to be absorbed.

CLARY SAGE: a relaxing, warming and almost euphoric effect, especially helpful where anxiety leads to exhaustion.

LAVENDER: calming, helping to balance the mind and emotions, it is one of the gentlest oils to use.

MELISSA: very soothing and, like Lavender, gentle to the skin.

It is useful where anxiety affects the digestion, and also where hormone imbalance creates tension (see Pre-menstrual Problems, page 71).

ROSE: it is wonderfully relaxing and is also considered one of the finest hormone regulators.

YLANG-YLANG: almost sedating, it slows the heart-rate and excessively rapid breathing. Do not overdo it, as large amounts or prolonged usage can result in a headache.

HERBALISM

Herbal remedies are well suited to relieving anxiety, try using one or more of the following herb teas:

CHAMOMILE *(Chamomilla recutita)*: relaxing and good for the digestion; tea bags of it are sold everywhere.

LEMON BALM *(Melissa officinalis)*: this can be safely taken over quite a time for mild anxiety; the fresh herb is much nicer tasting, just gather a few sprigs and take a tea morning and night.

LIME BLOSSOM *(Tilia europaea)*: a very good evening drink, to soothe the mind and calm the digestion and heart-rate.

SKULLCAP *(Scutellaria lateriflora)*: more strongly relaxing, this herb may be easier to find in tablet form.

VALERIAN *(Valeriana officinalis)*: a powerful relaxant, relieving mental and physical tension. Better to take in tablet form, or up to 5 ml (1 tsp) of the tincture, as the tea tastes disgusting!

HOMEOPATHY

As always, long-term problems need professional treatment. In the meantime, a choice of these remedies may help.

ACONITE: for a sudden onset of anxiety or fear, perhaps after a fright, with much restlessness.

ARGENTICUM NITRICUM: for tension giving rise to butterflies in the stomach and indigestion, or a constant craving for sweet things.

ARSENICUM ALBUM: if very restless, fearful, no appetite and very finicky about food.

GELSEMIUM: for nervous apprehension, such as pre-exam nerves or stage fright, with weak trembling knees.

NATUROPATHY

Apart from recommending activities like yoga or meditation to help reduce levels of anxiety in the long term, gentle exercise and warm baths may be helpful to ease tensions and calm down. The addition of a Vitamin B complex supplement in the mornings, and calcium in the evenings will help both to feed the nervous system and restore a more natural rhythm to the energy use through the day – one of the reasons for the popularity of milky drinks as a nightcap is that they are rich in calcium, a natural relaxant.

Lime Blossom tea

DEPRESSION

Just as with anxiety, depression can be due to several reasons, and its symptoms may be quite varied. Conditions like constipation, headaches, insomnia and loss of appetite can all relate to depression and in deep or continuing instances of depression professional help is essential. This is especially so when there is no obvious reason for the feelings, a condition generally labelled endogenous depression.

AROMATHERAPY

Many oils have quite profound effects on mood, and it may be necessary to change the oil used as symptoms vary. The benefits of aromatherapy massage using diluted essential oils (see page 17), with the caring effect of the direct contact, are the most useful way of treating someone with depression, but oils can also be very helpful in the bath (see page 8).

BERGAMOT: this is one of the most uplifting of oils, with a refreshing citrus fragrance which is appealing to both men and women – and gives Earl Grey tea its distinctive aroma.

CLARY SAGE: this is quite relaxing, but with an uplifting, almost euphoric effect as well; good when chronic tension has led to depression or exhaustion.

GERANIUM: this oil actually comes from varieties of scented pelargonium, and has a tonic effect on the adrenal cortex, which helps to regulate stress hormone production.

NEROLI: this oil, from the blossom of the bitter orange, is very concentrated (and also expensive!) so a little can go a long way. It relaxes and soothes, relieving muscle spasm and the irritability which often goes with a depressed state.

HERBALISM

The traditional approach to depression included looking at all the body systems, in particular liver function, and often bitter herbs were prescribed to stimulate digestion and

OATSTRAW (*Avena sativa*)

act as a tonic; a few drops of a tincture (see page 14) of a herb such as Gentian (*Gentiana lutea*) may do the trick in mild cases of depressed spirits. The herbs below can be taken as a tea, or for a stronger effect take as an infusion (see page 12).

BORAGE (*Borago officinalis*): an adrenal stimulant and general tonic, best taken as a tea and for short periods only.

OATSTRAW (*Avena sativa*): an all-round nervous restorative; either use 20 drops of the tincture twice daily, or simply add plenty of oats to the diet, for example, in cereals.

ROSEMARY (*Rosmarinus officinalis*): excellent where nervous exhaustion leads to depression, also good for headaches and sluggish digestion.

VERVAIN (*Verbena officinalis*): a relaxing tonic, very useful for the depression of convalescence from an illness, when everything seems a struggle.

HOMEOPATHY

In the short term, look at these remedies.

AURUM METALLICUM: for deep depression and almost suicidal feelings, perhaps following failure in exams or at work.

IGNATIA: this is especially appropriate for depression following a shock or grief, with pent-up, almost hysterical feelings and a lump in the throat .

KALI PHOS: for nervous exhaustion, leaving a lack of mental or physical energy.

PULSATILLA: generally most useful for mild, gentle people who are prone to weepiness, with a rapid change of mood to feeling miserable – this is often a good remedy for children, but seek medical advice first!

NATUROPATHY

One of the first things to do is overhaul the diet, to make sure there is enough nourishment for the nervous system. Reduce coffee, tea, sugar and alcohol intake. Take plenty of wholefoods, possibly increasing protein intake, if the diet has been poor.

Taking more exercise is a positive move, helping to improve circulation, muscle tone and increase oxygen intake. The main difficulty of course is motivation, so support from an exercise class may be more successful than doing it alone.

Supplement the diet with a good general multi-mineral and vitamin supplement to give a wide spectrum of nutrients.

HEADACHES

Headaches can develop for a number of reasons; usually they can be related to some obvious cause such as nasal congestion or sinusitis, eyestrain, fatigue or tension. The majority of headaches are due to stress or worries, with muscle spasms in the neck leading to head pains. These can be made worse by poor posture, and many jobs create special problems – for instance, computer operators often get eyestrain and stiff, aching shoulders or neck muscles, and consequently headaches.

AROMATHERAPY

Many essential oils have some analgesic properties. A useful way of employing the following for headaches is as a cold compress (see page 15), applied to the temples and forehead – use 5 drops in a small bowl of cold water, wring out a flannel or something similar and place on the area. Alternatively, gently massage a couple of drops directly into the temples.

LAVENDER: relaxing, warming and analgesic, one of the gentlest of oils. Where there is neck tension, apply a hot compress to the neck and upper back at the same time (proportions as above for cold compress).

PEPPERMINT: this is very cooling in its effect, and is also very useful for relieving catarrh and nasal congestion. As it has something of a stimulant action, it could be used in equal amounts with Lavender, as described above, on the temples and forehead.

ROSEMARY: this is even more stimulating to the central nervous system, and is excellent for headaches following

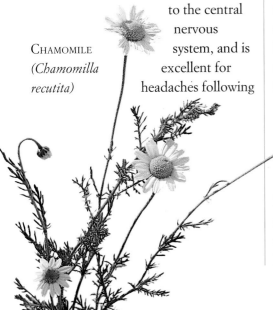

CHAMOMILE
(*Chamomilla recutita*)

SEVERE HEADACHES

Causes such as very high blood pressure, meningitis or even brain tumours are much rarer; these of course need professional treatment, and severe, unexplained or persistent headaches should be checked out carefully, but most headaches can be identified and cured at home. Where there has been any kind of accident, for instance a whiplash injury, it makes good sense to consult a manipulative therapist such as a chiropractor or an osteopath.

mental strain and exhaustion, as well as helping to clear the sinuses.

HERBALISM

At the earliest signs of a headache taking a herbal tea from the choice below can stop it in its tracks; if the headache is more pronounced, or is a repeated problem, try making an infusion (see page 12) for a stronger effect, or else get medical advice.

CHAMOMILE (*Chamomilla recutita*): good for bilious headaches, stemming from over-eating or indigestion, where there is a dull, throbbing pain on top of the head.

LIME BLOSSOM (*Tilia europaea*): soothes the nerves and is very helpful for tension headaches; can be mixed with Peppermint for a more uplifting effect.

PEPPERMINT
(*Mentha piperita*)

PEPPERMINT
(*Mentha piperita*): this works well for digestive or sinus headaches, especially where the head feels hot.

ROSEMARY (*Rosmarinus officinalis*): for headaches related to exhaustion or depression, and also for bilious heavy heads. When the headache is due to a hangover, Rosemary and Peppermint tea can do wonders – but prevention is still better than a cure!

HOMEOPATHY

The choice is large, in part due to the many factors which go to produce the individual symptoms.

For tension headaches, gently massage the temples with small circling movements.

BELLADONNA: for a burning, violent headache with a hot head; the symptoms are worse with any jarring movement of the head, or loud noises.

BRYONIA: for a severe, splitting headache, only relieved by lying very still or with firm, cool pressure across the forehead.

NUX VOMICA: for a sharp headache, either on waking or after food, with nausea or bilious feelings from over-eating; better if taken when lying down, and keeping warm.

PULSATILLA: good for headaches associated with menstruation, also where brought on by too much rich food; relief seems to come from cool applications to the head and being out in the fresh air.

Eating a varied diet of fresh vegetables and wholefoods can ward off many ailments.

NATUROPATHY

In general, the naturopathic approach is to look at prevention, by changing lifestyle to reduce the reasons for headaches. Eating a varied wholefood diet, reducing alcohol, coffee and tea, and getting more exercise and fresh air are all likely to help lower the frequency of headaches for regular sufferers. Drink plenty of fluids, as dehydration can be a factor, especially for people working in hot, stuffy atmospheres and, of course, in

BENEFITS OF SELF-HELP
Prevention is better than cure so try to adopt some of the measures outlined in this book to maintain good health rather than just waiting to be ill. If you suffer from several complaints, read all the relevant sections for an overall picture of what you can do to improve your general health and be aware of early signs of trouble.

hangovers. Avoid dramatic changes in diet, such as crash dieting, which upsets blood sugar levels and can contribute to headaches. Sometimes a Vitamin B complex supplement can be useful in relieving mental exhaustion. For hot, congested headaches use cold compresses to the forehead, perhaps combined with a hot footbath to improve circulation.

INSOMNIA

It is important to distinguish between habitual sleeplessness, repeated night after night, and a temporary problem due perhaps to some worry or anxiety. It is also important not to become obsessed with trying to get a certain amount of sleep; not everyone needs an 8-hour quota – quality is more vital than quantity. People generally need less sleep as they get older, or at least less continuously, so if granny has a day-time snooze and sleeps for less time at night, that is perfectly normal.

AROMATHERAPY

Essential oils are a very pleasant and effective means of unwinding and aiding restful sleep – try using them in the bath (see page 8) – or else putting 2-3 drops on to a paper tissue under the pillow at night. Choose from the following, either using a single oil or a blend; do not use the same oil for more than 2 weeks or you will find it becomes less effective.

CHAMOMILE: calming and relaxing in its effects, it is good where indigestion contributes to broken sleep.

CLARY SAGE: this has a sedating and almost euphoric action, *but* do not use if you have had alcohol as you can quickly get drunk, and have nightmares or a hangover feeling later on.

LAVENDER: not only very soothing, but also analgesic, so if any aches or pains contribute to insomnia, this oil is probably the best remedy.

MARJORAM: relaxing and warming, in large amounts it is quite sedating but can leave you feeling a bit thick-headed the next morning, so do not overdo it.

HERBALISM

An infusion (see page 12) of one or more of these relaxing herbs can help a return to a natural sleep pattern if stress has disturbed it. Other ways of using herbs include herb-filled pillows; traditionally hops were used as they are sedating (but not very pleasant-smelling!). Fill a small muslin bag loosely with the appropriate herb and place under your normal pillow.

Another old favourite remedy was cowslip wine; this not only tastes better than the infusion but is certainly very relaxing.

CHAMOMILE: *(Chamomilla recutita)*: calms the stomach and the brain, settling the digestion and helping sleep.

HYSSOP *(Hyssopus officinalis)*: a gentle relaxant; also helps to ease nasal congestion and colds, which can cause insomnia.

LEMON BALM *(Melissa officinalis)*: this helps to restore balance to the nervous system, and can be used safely on children. The fresh herb tastes much nicer, and can be drunk as a tea anytime.

LIME BLOSSOM *(Tilia europaea)*: mildly analgesic as well as calming; can soothe headache or other pains.

PASSIONFLOWER *(Passiflora incarnata)*: a strong relaxant or sedative, but without any ill-effects. Many commercial herbal tablets for insomnia contain this herb.

HOMEOPATHY

In the short term, look at these remedies:

ACONITE: for restlessness associated with sudden upset or fear, and resulting in tossing and turning in bed.

COFFEA: if the mind is completely awake and the brain will not turn off – just as if you had drunk strong coffee.

Probably the most versatile and useful essential oil is Lavender, distilled from the flowers.

NUX VOMICA: for insomnia due to overwork or excess food or alcohol, waking around 3 or 4 a.m. for several hours, with disturbed dreams.

SULPHUR: for over-excitement, with the mind full of ideas, and easily awakened by the slightest noise.

NATUROPATHY

In order to get the proper rhythm of energy through the day, it is useful to get plenty of exercise and get fresh air in the daytime. It may help to get up fairly early in the morning as well, to restore this balance. Do not sleep in a stuffy room, or drink coffee, tea or cola at night.

At bedtime, a calcium/magnesium supplement such as dolomite tablets can help to relax, especially if taken with a warm herb tea, or perhaps a hot milky drink if you do not suffer from a lot of catarrh.

MIGRAINE

Anyone who has experienced a migraine will know that it is more than a severe headache. Migraines generally involve acute pains, often over one eye, and perhaps disturbed vision or flashing lights. There may also be nausea or vomiting, and sensitivity to bright light.

AROMATHERAPY

Since the sense of smell is altered and often heightened during a migraine, aromatherapy is definitely best used between attacks; use at the earliest stage of a migraine only if the smell is well tolerated.

A central feature of the natural approach to migraines is to distinguish between a "hot" migraine, where the blood vessels are dilated, and a "cold" migraine, where there is excessive constriction of the blood vessels. In the first type, a cold or perhaps just cool compress (see page 15) across the forehead will give relief and oils of Peppermint or Lavender can be used. For "cold" types of migraine, a hot compress on the forehead or back of the neck may help, using Marjoram.

HERBALISM

Catching the migraine early gives the best chance of success (otherwise try to use these infusions regularly, as a preventive). Choose from the following:

CHAMOMILE (*Chamomilla recutita*): for dull, throbbing headache with a feeling of queasiness – add a little Ginger (*Zingiber officinalis*) to relieve more severe nausea.

FEVERFEW (*Chrysanthemum parthenium*): an excellent remedy taken daily to prevent the "cold" type of migraine, where there is a sense of a tight band around the head. This is widely available in tablet form as well.

ROSEMARY (*Rosmarinus officinalis*): good where stress is a trigger for migraines, and where local warmth gives relief.

CAUSES OF MIGRAINE
A migraine can be triggered by all sorts of factors: hormone changes, stress, stuffy atmospheres, noises, smells and certain foods are well-known triggers. Repeated attacks call for professional help; self-help treatments should be largely used as preventive measures.

HOMEOPATHY

During an attack try one of these:

KALI BICH: for an intense headache, preceded by a loss of vision and nausea, made worse in hot weather.

NATRUM MURIATICUM: for a severe, pounding headache with zigzags in front of the eyes, nausea and a pale face. The migraine may also be triggered by menstruation.

SILICA: for pains spreading from the back of the neck over to the eyes, usually right-sided, and often vomiting.

NATUROPATHY

Diet needs to be looked at carefully; try to avoid tea, coffee, alcohol especially red wine, red meat, cheese, chocolate, tomatoes and eggs. Eat plenty of fresh, raw salads and drink lots of fluid, as dehydration can be a factor. Try taking a Vitamin B supplement daily and see if this helps to reduce attacks. In between attacks, exercises to relieve tension in the neck and shoulders can be useful, and also massage of these areas (see left).

NECK MASSAGE FOR MIGRAINE

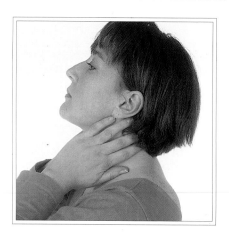

1 For stiff, aching neck muscles massage the neck with firm circular movements. Try to keep the arms relaxed.

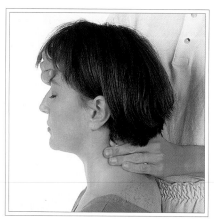

2 Ideally get someone else to massage the neck for you. They can also support your head while they massage.

NEURALGIA

Neuralgia is a sharp pain originating along the course of one or more nerves, and may come about from a variety of causes; both sciatica and shingles (see pages 26 and 27) give rise to forms of neuralgic pain. Facial neuralgia, affecting one of the trigeminal nerves in the face, can give intense pain, and may relate to stress, migraines or dental problems.

AROMATHERAPY

Using warm compresses (see page 15), including analgesic oils, over the affected areas can give much relief. Choose from Chamomile, Lavender, Marjoram or Rosemary oils – alternate the oil used for recurrent pains, or blend them together for greater effect.

HERBALISM

An infusion (see page 12) of Lavender *(Lavandula vera)* flowers, Lime Blossom *(Tilia europaea)* and Rosemary *(Rosmarinus officinalis)* leaves can be very helpful, not only to ease the pains but to ease tension and tone the nervous system. This mixture can also be used as a warm compress directly over the area.

Two other helpful herbs as infusions are:

St John's Wort *(Hypericum perforatum)*: anti-inflammatory and a nervous restorative. The blood-red oil made by infusing the flowers in pure vegetable oil

VERVAIN
(Verbena officinalis)

(see page 13) is an excellent local analgesic and healer.

Vervain *(Verbena officinalis)*: a relaxant and nervous tonic, very helpful when neuralgia is related to being generally run-down and exhausted.

HOMEOPATHY

In the short term, try the following:

Actaea rac: for facial neuralgia with pains into the cheekbone and as if piercing the eyeball. Pains ease at night.

Belladonna: for a hot, burning and flushed face, with mostly right-sided neuralgic pains and twitching muscles.

Rosemary *(Rosmarinus officinalis)*

Gelsemium: for pains radiating from the neck into the face, possibly with some nausea; migraine-related neuralgia.

NATUROPATHY

Simply using alternating hot and cold compresses, 3-4 minutes hot and a maximum 1 minute cold, repeated a few times, can ease the pains. For chronic sufferers a Vitamin B complex supplement can help to nourish the nervous system. In addition, look at ways of reducing stress such as relaxation or yoga classes.

SCIATICA

Pains along some point of the sciatic nerves, running from the low back down either leg to the foot, are a common form of neuralgia (see page 25). The pains may come about from an injury, and treatment from an osteopath or chiropractor should always be considered as one of the best ways to correct the cause. Poor posture, badly designed chairs or even a full back pocket can all cause pressure and pain in the sciatic nerve.

AROMATHERAPY

Initially, use cold compresses (see page 15) with either Chamomile or Lavender oils included. When the pains are less acute, or in longer-lasting sciatic discomfort, try warm compresses as suggested for Neuralgia (see page 25).

These oils are very helpful, diluted 2 per cent in a base oil and slowly massaged into the affected area.

HERBALISM

Chamomile (*Chamomilla recutita*) or Lavender (*Lavandula vera*) are also two useful herbs to take in infusion (see page 12) to ease muscle spasm and inflammation which add to the pains. For acute muscle spasms in the thigh or legs, try making a strong decoction (see page 12) of Cramp Bark (European Cranberry Bush) (*Viburnum opulus*) and using as a warm compress. A small cupful of this may be taken internally as a powerful relaxant.

CRAMP BARK (EUROPEAN CRANBERRY BUSH)
(*Viburnum opulus*)

IMPROVING YOUR POSTURE

Apart from the suggestions listed on this page, you may want to consider help with improving your posture, learning how to move and hold yourself comfortably. The Alexander Technique and the Feldenkrais Technique are two systems that can help here; there are many qualified teachers of both available. Massage is not generally suitable in an acute phase, but in the longer term it is very helpful (see below for self-massage, or find a good massage therapist for best results).

HOMEOPATHY

ARSEN ALB: for intermittent pains shooting from the thigh down to the knee or even ankle.
IGNATIA: for sharp pains in the lower back and upper thighs, eased by walking around.
RHUS TOX: for severe pains in the hip, radiating down to the knee and causing limping. Generally these pains are worse in damp weather.

NATUROPATHY

Hot and cold compresses, as described for Neuralgia (see page 25), may give relief. Gentle exercise is generally useful, but stop if it becomes too painful. Take a serious look at your posture, how you bend, pick things up and so on. It is important to try to keep your back fairly upright, using your legs

LAVENDER
(*Lavandula 'Nana'*)

to bend or to take the weight.

Look carefully at all the chairs you use. Sit well back on a chair, and use cushions if necessary to get you into a more comfortable position. In general, avoid staying in one position for too long, as the muscles begin to tighten and stiffen. For example, try to have regular breaks on a long car journey, or walk about for a while on the train.

To help ease sciatic pain, massage diluted essential oils, as recommended, into the buttock and upper thigh with slow circular movements.

SHINGLES

This condition is brought about by the same virus, *Herpes zoster*, that causes chickenpox; it can lie dormant in the body for years before triggering an attack, often when you are stressed and exhausted. There is usually some pain in the affected area for a day or so before the very painful blisters appear along the pathway of the affected nerves. Sometimes there is considerable pain around the site for weeks, months or even years after the blisters have gone, and this can be treated in the same way as Neuralgia (see page 25).

AROMATHERAPY

A number of essential oils can act locally very powerfully to reduce the pains, dry up the blisters and as direct anti-viral agents. It may be best to use a combination of two or three of these oils; for small areas of blisters paint the oils on neat, once or twice daily, otherwise use them in the bath or diluted in water as a warm compress (see page 15).

Initially, choose from Bergamot, Eucalyptus or Tea Tree oils; if pains persist, use Lavender for its healing and analgesic properties – good combinations are Bergamot and Tea Tree, Bergamot and Lavender, but all the above are useful.

HERBALISM

Lavender oil *(Lavandula vera)*, as described above, is excellent for local use; this can be backed up by taking Lavender flowers as an infusion (see page 12) for their relaxing effect. If there are long-standing pains, after the acute attack has gone (known as post-herpetic syndrome), then a general nerve tonic like Oatstraw *(Avena sativa)* is very helpful – either take 20 drops of the tincture (see page 14) twice daily, or simply include plenty of oats in the diet, for instance as porridge. If depression has set in, an infusion of Rosemary *(Rosmarinus officinalis)* works wonders; drink a cupful in the morning. At the other end of the day, a cup of Lime Blossom *(Tilia europaea)* tea in the evening can help restful sleep.

LAVENDER *(Lavandula vera)*

HOMEOPATHY

Some possibilities are:

APIS MEL: where there is a large amount of blistering, with swelling and a burning sensation. Symptoms are eased by cold applications.

ARSEN ALB: for reddened skin, with the blisters merging together and possibly discharging. Symptoms eased by warm applications.

RHUS TOX: for highly inflamed skin, with small white blisters that are intensely painful and itchy; difficult to keep still due to the irritation and discomfort.

NATUROPATHY

In preventive terms, it is advisable to try to steer clear of someone with chickenpox, especially if you are feeling very run-down yourself. Since in real life you may be the one looking after your child with chickenpox, this is not so easy! Spraying the sick room with essential oils (see Aromatherapy above for choice), using 10-15 drops in a 600 ml (1 pt/2½ cups) plant spray filled with water, can help too.

If you feel the first signs of irritation, try rubbing the area with a freshly cut lemon. During an attack of shingles a salt bath may give relief and promote healing and drying of the blisters. Take a Vitamin B complex supplement to nourish the nervous system, and look generally at reducing stress and maintaining a healthy lifestyle.

STRESS

Stress is one of those rather vague terms that is very difficult to define. It is also important to say that stress is not in itself harmful, and a certain amount can be necessary to get us motivated and enjoying life; only when the amount of stress is too much for our systems to cope with does it become a problem. People have a marvellous capacity to adapt to and cope with various sources of stress, but when they get overloaded and nervous or adrenal exhaustion sets in, they can become seriously ill.

AROMATHERAPY

Many oils are of value in helping to reduce the impact of stress. The best way of using them is probably diluted in a vegetable oil and used in massage (see page 17), but if you do not have a willing, and trained, partner then use them in the bath (see page 8).

For more uplifting effects choose from Bergamot, Clary Sage, Geranium or Rosemary, while Lavender or Marjoram are more relaxing. Three luxurious, although expensive, oils which have excellent de-stressing properties (and smell wonderful!) are Jasmine, Neroli (or Orange Blossom) and Rose – use sparingly as they are very concentrated. Jasmine is relaxing and almost euphoric, Neroli is an anti-depressant and is refreshing, and Rose is calming and relaxing.

HERBALISM

For the more agitated aspects of being stressed, choose relaxing infusions such as Lavender (*Lavandula*

SYMPTOMS OF STRESS

Symptoms of stress vary, see also Anxiety and Depression (pages 19 and 20), but if you experience some or all of the following, you may be over-stressed:

❦ Constantly on edge, with a very short fuse and ready to explode for no real reason.

❦ Feeling on the verge of tears much of the time.

❦ Difficulty in concentrating, decision-making or with memory.

❦ Always tired even after a full night's sleep.

❦ Sleep itself is disturbed and unrefreshing.

❦ A feeling of not being able to cope, it's all too much.

❦ Poor appetite, or else nibbling without hunger.

❦ No sense of fun or enjoyment in life.

❦ Mistrustful of everybody, unable to enjoy company.

❦ Inability to relax or unwind even if not working.

❦ Problems in relationships, no interest in sex.

❦ Always fidgeting or having a nervous habit such as biting your nails or chewing your hair.

The first step to improving the situation is to recognize that you are stressed, and to know what your limits are. Taking active steps to reduce the amount of external stress will of course be helpful, as well as looking at the methods below for easing the effects of the stress on your system. Other steps might include trying a class in relaxation techniques, or yoga, T'ai Ch'i and so on, or having professional massage treatments. Getting regular breaks from a stressful lifestyle will help you to cope better and avoid the situation reaching a crisis point.

vera), Lime Blossom *(Tilia europaea)* or Lemon Balm *(Melissa officinalis),* or for acute tensions try Valerian *(Valeriana officinalis)* – since this tastes disgusting, it may be better to buy it in tablet form. When exhaustion has set in, infusions of Rosemary *(Rosmarinus officinalis),* Vervain *(Verbena officinalis)* or Betony *(Stachys betonica),* or a mixture of all three, will act as a tonic. Oats are

helpful to add to the diet, as a nourishment for the nervous system.

HOMEOPATHY

ACONITE: for acute anxiety and mental confusion, with thoughts whizzing round in the head and much restlessness.

CHAMOMILLA: if everything and everybody seems to irritate, and it is

GERANIUM
(Pelargonium graveolens)

MASSAGE FOR STIFF NECKS

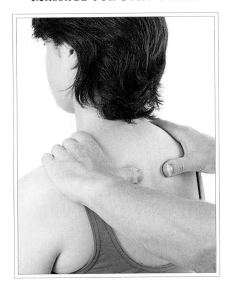

1 Place hands on each shoulder, thumbs on either side of the spine.

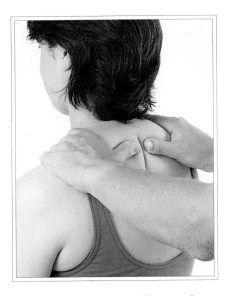

2 Rotate thumbs firmly, lifting and squeezing the shoulder muscles. Relax hands and repeat.

BACK MASSAGE TO EASE STRESS

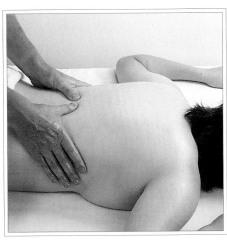

1 To relieve stress and tension, use effleurage, or stroking, on the back. Oil the back and then place hands on lower back with thumbs on either side of the spine.

2 Steadily stroke up the back, allow thumbs to move out at the shoulders to join the fingers, and stroke down the side of the back. Bring thumbs to either side of the spine and repeat several times in a slow, relaxing rhythm. Keep the pressure firm, but not too hard.

NECK AND SHOULDER EXERCISES

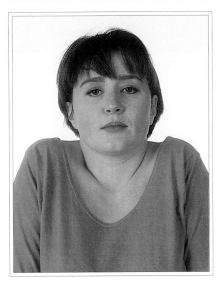

1 Lift shoulders, pressing into the neck Relax and then repeat a few times.

2 Roll the shoulders in a circle. Repeat a few times in a backwards circle, then a few times forwards.

very easy to get into a temper.

IGNATIA: for mood swings, liable to tears and lots of sighing; may bottle things up and get upset suddenly.

KALI PHOS: for prolonged strain, getting fatigued and rather depressed, very jumpy at the least thing. Tends to withdraw from company, doesn't want to go out very much, generally lacks interest in life.

NATUROPATHY

A good plan is to look at basics; overhaul the diet, cutting out all the stimulants such as coffee, tea or cola drinks which only serve to leave you more exhausted when their effects wear off. Also reduce alcohol; it may help you to relax in small amounts but it easily becomes a dangerous habit and has a depressant action in any quantity.

Try to get some exercise; this not only helps to use up excess adrenalin but builds up physical *and* mental stamina. Deeper breathing will also supply more oxygen to the brain, which is the first essential nourishment it needs. It may be useful to add a multi-vitamin and mineral supplement to the diet for a while, as the body uses up nutrients faster when under stress.

The Respiratory System

In order to prevent respiratory problems, or to help clear them up more quickly, it is essential to take a wider, holistic view of health. If you live in a relatively mild, damp climate, this will make you more prone to respiratory infections and catarrh; coupled with this, the increase in air pollution this century has added significantly to the burden. However, some internal factors, such as diet, exercise and general health, are also important in affecting our resistance to infections, and the more we pay attention to these internal factors, the healthier we will be.

Breathing is one of those bodily functions that normally carry on automatically, but can also be controlled consciously. This is a good illustration of the effect of stress and anxiety on our body, as shallow or over-rapid breathing, nervous coughs and even bronchial spasms can be produced when in an agitated state. Poor posture, lack of exercise or just lack of fresh air, smoking or smoky atmospheres all contribute to an inadequate intake of oxygen and respiratory problems.

ABOVE: The influence of essential oils on our respiratory system can have dramatic effects. Very many essential oils are also extremely pleasing to smell and can help to keep the sinuses clear, for example Lavender (above left), Peppermint and Eucalyptus.

ASTHMA

Asthma is not generally a problem that should simply be tackled at home; it requires professional treatment and attention. Childhood asthma tends to be associated with an allergic response; there may also be hay fever and/or eczema present in the family. In trying to identify the allergens responsible it is often valuable to look further at external factors and also internal ones such as diet, as well as conventional skin testing.

AROMATHERAPY

During an actual attack of asthma, simply sniffing the aroma of a couple of drops of essential oil on a paper tissue may give relief from the spasm of the airways – choose from Lavender, Bergamot, Frankincense or Chamomile. In between attacks, massaging a choice of the above oils, diluted (see page 17), into the chest may help to prevent the spasms and build-up of thick mucus which gives the wheezing symptoms.

Essential oils, diluted in a base oil as recommended, can be massaged into the chest to relax the airways and ease breathing.

HERBALISM

Professional practitioners may use remedies which directly reduce the allergic response, or dilate the bronchial passageways, depending

CHAMOMILE
(Chamomilla recutita)

EYEBRIGHT *(Euphrasia officinalis)*

on specific individual needs. In between asthma attacks, taking an infusion (see page 12) of a mixture of Chamomile *(Chamomilla recutita)*, Eyebright *(Euphrasia officinalis)* and Lavender *(Lavandula vera)* may help to relax the airways, tone up the mucous membranes and reduce inflammation and irritability of the bronchi.

HOMEOPATHY

The professional will similarly look to treat each person individually, so only consider the remedies below in the short term:

ACONITE: at the earliest sign of breathing problems, especially if brought on by a cold, or simply cold weather with strong winds, and where there is much anxiety or fear.

ARSENICUM: when symptoms are worse after midnight, with restlessness and a feeling of exhaustion.

IPECACUANHA: where

there is wheezing, with a persistent, rattly cough accompanied by a strong feeling of nausea.

NATUROPATHY

For childhood asthma, or where there is a lot of thick mucus, it is well worth trying a change of diet, to exclude cows' milk products for a while, to decrease sugary baking products and sweets (candy), and to increase fresh vegetables and fruit.

Breathing exercises may be of help, especially for later-onset asthma or when exercise seems to aggravate the condition; a simple method of deepening the breathing pattern is to

A useful breathing exercise for asthma is simply to blow up a couple of balloons a day, to deepen the breath and exercise the diaphragm.

BREATHING EXERCISES

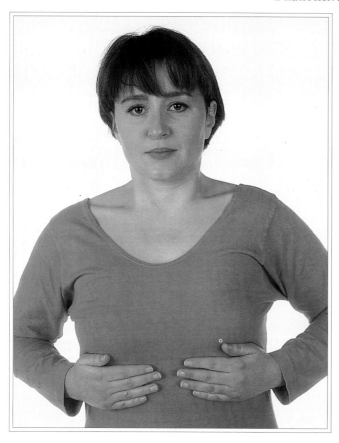

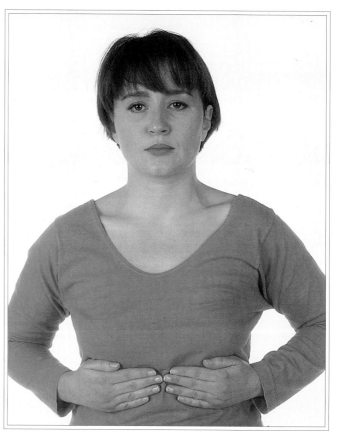

1 Place hands just below the breastbone and take a slow, deep breath. As you breathe in, push out the stomach; this should make the hands move apart a little, as the diaphragm moves.

2 As you breathe out, pull the stomach in. The diaphragm moves back up and the hands come together again. Repeat just 3 or 4 times and then breathe normally.

blow up balloons – for a maximum effect blow them up until they burst! Regular back massage will help release muscle tensions and improve circulation. Using hot and cold compresses (see page 15) on the upper back and/or chest will also stimulate circulation through the lungs and help remove mucus.

FRENCH LAVENDER
(*Lavandula stoechas*)

To stimulate circulation into the back and chest, and loosen phlegm in the lungs, place hands in a cupped shape on the upper back and briskly move them alternately up

and down. This should make a hollow sound on the back – slapping is not helpful, or enjoyable! (Be prepared for some coughing if the chest is congested.)

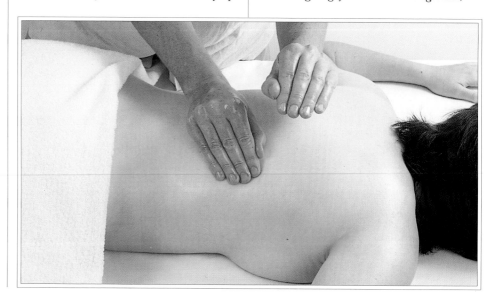

BRONCHITIS

Acute bronchitis, which typically follows an upper respiratory infection such as a heavy cold or influenza, produces a painful dry cough as the infected bronchi become inflamed. This leads to lots of mucus being produced and the cough becoming looser. The condition can recur, and chronic bronchitis is known as the "English disease" due to its frequent occurrence in England.

AROMATHERAPY

Essential oils, used primarily in steam inhalations (see below), are an excellent way to treat bronchitis. In the acute stage using powerfully antiseptic oils such as Lavender, Eucalyptus, Thyme or Tea Tree will be very useful. This can be backed up by gently rubbing a little diluted Lavender oil on to the chest – use 5 drops in 5ml (1 tsp) of olive oil or similar vegetable oil.

For more chronic symptoms choose from one of the following oils which are derived from gums or resins, or simply combine all three in an inhalation.
BENZOIN: is most famous as the ingredient in Friar's Balsam; it has a warming and relaxing effect on the bronchi, and aids expectoration of the thick mucus.

To make an inhalation, choose a bowl large enough to take at least 600 ml (1 pt/2½ cups) of water. Fill it with boiling water and add 2-3 drops of essential oil. As the oils vaporize, inhale the steam as deeply as possible. If you hold a towel over your head this will delay the effects of evaporation. Be careful to place the bowl in a safe position.

SELF-HELP MEASURES
There may not be any infection present in the chronic state; repeated irritation of the lungs produces excess mucus which clogs up the bronchi. Self-help measures include not smoking or being in smoky atmospheres, treating colds and so on promptly, not going out in foggy weather, and using steam inhalations to warm and moisten the airways.

FRANKINCENSE: another expectorant, which slows and deepens the breathing as well as being a good antiseptic agent.
MYRRH: strongly anti-infective, helping to loosen the sticky mucus and shift it off the chest.

HERBALISM

There is a whole treasure chest of herbal medicines for different stages or states of bronchitis; if in doubt do seek professional advice. At the beginning, where there may be a feeling of chill, a tea from fresh Ginger (*Zingiber officinalis*) with perhaps a pinch of Cayenne pepper added will give warmth very quickly. Painful, harsh coughs can be soothed with infusions of Marshmallow leaf (*Althea officinalis*), Hyssop (*Hyssopus officinalis*) and Thyme (*Thymus vulgaris*), or else use White Horehound (*Marrubium vulgare*), an anti-spasmodic and expectorant remedy. A regular intake

of garlic, ideally fresh, not only helps to stimulate the removal of excess mucus in chronic bronchitis, but is one of the most powerful anti-infective agents there is, helping to build resistance to all respiratory infections.

HOMEOPATHY

In the acute phase, look at these remedies, but seek qualified treatment if symptoms persist or chest pains set in.
ACONITE: for use in the early stages, with painful, dry cough and much restlessness, with a slight fever.
BRYONIA: for a dry, hacking cough which is made worse by changes in temperature, such as coming into a warm room.
IPECACUANHA: for a spasmodic cough with much rattly mucus on the chest, and a tendency towards vomiting.
PHOSPHORUS: for a hoarse voice, even going altogether, and a dry tickly cough, with a tight feeling like a band around the chest.

NATUROPATHY

Reduce mucus-forming foods: these are primarily dairy products, and also refined carbohydrates such as cakes and pastries. If the weather is damp or foggy, stay indoors, but also avoid rooms being too dry and hot. In chronic cases walking or other exercise in good weather will improve breathing. Hot and cold compresses (see page 15) will really stimulate circulation through the lungs and help breathing.

CATARRH

Irritation of the membranes of the nose and throat will encourage production of mucus; where this becomes excessive or prolonged, for example after a cold, then catarrh is the result. When this occurs lower down the airways, bronchial catarrh follows (see Bronchitis, page 33). Nasal catarrh is even more common in damp climates and the same advice is applicable.

AROMATHERAPY

Where there is a lot of nasal congestion, a steam inhalation with essential oils (see page 33) can be instantly effective in giving relief. In the short term Peppermint is excellent, especially combined with Eucalyptus and/or Tea Tree, to loosen thick, sticky mucus and fight any infection present. For longer term catarrhal problems, try using oil of Pine instead of Peppermint, perhaps with Chamomile, Lavender or Tea Tree.

HERBALISM

Apart from using steam inhalations for temporary relief, either with oils as described above or using a handful each of Peppermint (*Mentha piperita*) leaves, Eucalyptus (*Eucalyptus globulus*) leaves and Chamomile (*Chamomilla*

recutita) flowers to 1 litre (1¾ pt/4 cups) of boiling water, catarrh can often be very successfully treated with infusions (see page 12) of the following:

CATMINT (*Nepeta cataria*): helps to ease nasal congestion and improve the circulation through the nasal passages.

ELDERFLOWER (*Sambucus nigra*): has an anti-inflammatory effect, reducing swelling of the membranes and easing mucus production.

GOLDEN ROD (*Solidago virgaurea*): astringent, toning up the membranes and also reducing excess mucus.

HYSSOP (*Hyssopus officinalis*): loosens up thick phlegm, while calming the breathing; good if there is restlessness and problems with sleeping due to difficulty in breathing.

HOMEOPATHY

Initially think of one of these remedies:

ARSEN ALB: for running, watery catarrh, with a dripping nose.

HYDRASTIS: for a constant post-nasal drip, perhaps associated with blocked Eustachian tubes (connecting to the middle ear), creating a little deafness.

KALI BICH: where there is thick, stringy mucus, which is difficult to shift.

PULSATILLA: in chronic cases, where the catarrh varies at times from clear to a greenish-yellow colour.

Place 25 g (1 oz) dried Chamomile (Chamomilla recutita) leaves in a teapot and pour on boiling water. Allow to infuse for 5 minutes. Strain and drink a cupful.

GOLDEN ROD (*Solidago virgaurea*)

NATUROPATHY

Avoid all mucus-forming foods, especially milk and other dairy products, and refined carbohydrates – most breakfasts of cereal and milk fall into this category, as do pastries, cakes and so on. Drinking warm fruit juices can often be helpful. If the catarrh tends to follow on from regular colds, a daily supplement of Vitamin C, up to 500 mg in strength, may need to be taken for a while.

Regular intake of garlic is invaluable in building up resistance to respiratory infections – ideally raw – and since the smell may stop other people coming near you, so colds are harder to catch! Actually, the smelly oil is the most anti-infective part of garlic, and 99 per cent of it is excreted out via the lungs so it works very strongly on the respiratory system. Odourless garlic perles, or capsules, will also work, although not as powerfully as the raw ingredient.

COLDS

Since there are over 200 strains of cold virus, it is not surprising that a cure has not been found. Prevention is better than treatment by far; once a cold has developed, it generally has to run its course. However, treatments can help to relieve symptoms and also stop the cold turning into persistent catarrh or a deeper infection.

AROMATHERAPY

Two methods are most appropriate for using oils to combat cold symptoms and stop complications: steam inhalations (see page 33) and baths. If, in the early stages, the cold is accompanied by a chill, adding 10 drops of Lavender and 5 drops of Cinnamon oil to a warm bath at night will help a lot. More stimulating oils such as Eucalyptus or Tea Tree (10 drops of each) can be used in baths earlier in the day. All the above are valuable in inhalations; a mixture often works better than just one oil.

GINGER (*Zingiber officinalis*)

HERBALISM

One of the herbalists' most traditional standbys for colds is still one of the best: use an infusion (see page 12) of equal amounts of Peppermint (*Mentha piperita*), Elderflower (*Sambucus nigra*) and Yarrow (*Achillea millefolium*). Taken hot just before going to bed, this will induce a sweat, and if the cold is caught early enough, may stop it altogether. Even if too late for this, it will still be

very useful. Other herbs that may be added to the infusion include:
CAYENNE (*Capsicum minimum*): a favourite North American Indian remedy: use 1.25 ml (¼ tsp) of the powder to really stimulate the circulation.
CINNAMON (*Cinnamomum zeylanicum*): use a cinnamon stick, and break it into the mixture of herbs, for a gentle, warming and sweat-inducing effect.
GINGER (*Zingiber officinalis*): grate a small piece of fresh root ginger into the mixture for extra heat.

HOMEOPATHY

ACONITE: for early stages of colds, when starting suddenly, perhaps after exposure to cold winds.
GELSEMIUM: for influenza-like symptoms, feeling chilly and trembling but with a flushed face.
NAT MUR: when there is a lot of sneezing, the nose is sore and inflamed and producing lots of mucus, either watery or like raw egg-white.

Fresh fruit is a natural source of Vitamin C.

CINNAMON (*Cinnamomum zeylanicum*)

NATUROPATHY

Immediately increase Vitamin C intake; at the earliest stages very high doses of a Vitamin C supplement, up to 2,000 mg, may stop the infection alone, but if left too late, this is not needed and may make the bowels too loose. 500 mg is an ample dose to take regularly until the remaining symptoms clear up. Another useful supplement is sucking zinc lozenges, with up to 20 mg zinc gluconate in them, every 3-4 hours initially (taking *tablets* does not have the same effect).

Eat lots of fresh fruit for natural Vitamin A, B and C, and add plenty of raw garlic to food. Cut out sugary, starchy or milky foods. A short cleansing diet of just fresh fruit and salads, and plenty of liquids such as warm fruit juices or herb teas, will encourage the body to throw off the cold more effectively.

COUGHS

A cough is a natural reflex reaction to any irritation, inflammation or blockage in the airways. It often accompanies an infection such as a cold or bronchitis, but may come about through nervousness, with no direct irritation at all. By keeping the bronchial tubes open and clear, coughing can be of vital importance, and treatment should generally be aimed first at making the cough more effective rather than just suppressing it.

AROMATHERAPY

A useful way to help a cough do its job more effectively is by using oils in a steam inhalation (see page 33); oils can be chosen to soothe the lining of the air passages, fight infection if needed, and loosen mucus to make it easier to be removed.

Soothing oils include Benzoin and Lavender. Many essential oils are antiseptic, especially Thyme and Eucalyptus; to increase expectoration choose Frankincense or Marjoram. In fact all the above oils are helpful for tackling coughs. Choose a blend that you like the smell of – and remember that if the cough does not improve within a few days, seek professional help, especially for children.

THYME *(Thymus vulgaris)*

HERBALISM

This is an area where herbs are of special benefit; if in doubt get qualified treatment. Choose from one or a mixture of the following, taken as warm infusions (see page 12).

COLTSFOOT *(Tussilago farfara)*: one of the best cough remedies, particularly for irritating, spasmodic coughs. It will soothe, loosen mucus and reduce the spasm.

HYSSOP *(Hyssopus officinalis)*: a calming and relaxing expectorant, when the cough is

Fresh or dried herbs can be used to make a steam inhalation, to loosen congested mucus and open the airways.

associated with restlessness and irritation.

MARSHMALLOW *(Althea officinalis)*: a demulcent remedy, which means it is highly soothing to the inflamed tubes. For a harsh, dry and painful cough always include Marshmallow in a mixture, to ease the soreness.

THYME *(Thymus vulgaris)*: powerfully antiseptic, this relieves a dry cough linked with a respiratory infection.

WHITE HOREHOUND *(Marrubium vulgare)*: an expectorant, freeing up thick, sticky mucus and helping it to be removed more effectively.

TYPES OF COUGH

It can be useful to divide coughs into two types; when the membranes are hot and dry the cough is painful and non-productive. As mucus is produced, the cough becomes moist, looser and can feel almost choking. The first kind needs soothing, while the latter requires help in removing the excess mucus. Choose the appropriate treatments in each case.

HOMEOPATHY

For short-term treatment of a cough, try a few doses (see page 10) of one of these remedies:

ACONITE: for a dry, short cough which may occur first thing in the morning, or come on after exposure to cold, dry winds.

BRYONIA: for a really spasmodic, dry cough which shakes the whole body and is worse with movement or after eating.

IPECACUANHA: for a moist cough, with some wheezing and a feeling of choking, and often much nausea.

PHOSPHORUS: for a dry, irritating and tickly cough, made worse by changes in temperature.

NATUROPATHY

Initially coughs are often quite dry and painful; taking a little honey from a spoon will help to soothe this. To make the honey much more powerful, try mashing a little chopped raw onion or garlic into it first; it is anti-social but very effective! Cut out all dairy products from the diet, to reduce the catarrh.

Either steam inhalations or a hot compress (see page 15) will encourage expectoration and stimulate the lungs to work better.

Once a cough has been eased, try not to slip back into eating patterns which include a lot of sugar, dairy products, cakes or pastries, as this can lower resistance to infection and help the cough to linger on or even to return in full force.

Fields of commercially-grown lavender.

GARLIC (*Allium sativum*)

For children, and for anybody where the cause is unknown, when the cough persists it is important to seek medical advice, as professional help may be needed. Similarly, if the mucus is bright green or yellow this indicates the presence of an infection, and advice should be sought.

EARACHE

Earaches most often develop through an infection, perhaps following a cold or sinusitis, for instance. Because infections can spread through into the middle or even inner ear, with potentially serious complications, earaches should not be neglected. If an earache is associated with catarrh, this should be treated too. Do *not* put anything into the ear unless it has been examined to ensure that the eardrum is not perforated.

AROMATHERAPY

Use hot compresses (see page 15) over the ear to draw the inflammation outwards, and hopefully help any pus that may be present to come out also. Two very good oils to use are Chamomile and Lavender; a combination of both may be most effective.

HERBALISM

Hot compresses are the most effective home treatment; Chamomile (*Chamomilla recutita*) may be used as an infusion (see page 12) for this purpose too. Taking garlic internally will help to reduce any catarrh and fight infection – if on proper examination the eardrum is not perforated, then a clove of garlic can be crushed into 5 ml (1 tsp) of olive oil; this is warmed to blood temperature and a few drops gently inserted into the ear for an excellent local antibiotic.

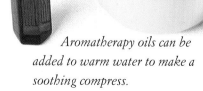

Aromatherapy oils can be added to warm water to make a soothing compress.

BELLADONNA *(Atropa belladonna)*

HOMEOPATHY

As acute remedies only, choose from the following:
BELLADONNA: for throbbing pains, with a flushed face, a lot of heat around the ear and perhaps a high temperature.
HEPAR SULPH: for a very painful ear, very tender to touch, and which may be discharging offensive pus – this situation requires medical attention quite quickly so do not let it go on unchecked.
PULSATILLA: if there is a lot of thick, green catarrh present, and the earache and congestion is worse in hot rooms or stuffy atmospheres.

NATUROPATHY

Apart from all the local treatments by compress suggested above, follow the advice given for Catarrh (see page 34), especially if there is a pattern of recurring earaches, as prevention should be the primary aim.

CHAMOMILE *(Chamomilla recutita)*

HAY FEVER

Hay fever is an allergic reaction, which can be triggered not just by grass pollens but in some people by various flower or tree pollens too. It is often seen together with other allergic reactions such as asthma and/or eczema, and if it is not relieved by the suggested self-help approaches, then seek qualified treatment. Practitioners may well start to act preventively before the hay fever season.

AROMATHERAPY

Simply sniffing a drop or two of an essential oil may be the best method; steam inhalations (see page 33) can be used but might be too hot for some people. You may well need to vary the oils used through the hay fever season, as they can become less effective if used for too long. Choose from Chamomile, Tea Tree, Pine, Melissa or Eucalyptus.

HERBALISM

Two herbs are very helpful in reducing the symptoms of hay fever: Chamomile (*Chamomilla recutita*) and Eyebright (*Euphrasia officinalis*).

Make an infusion of Chamomile (Chamomilla recutita), *when cool soak a couple of cotton pads and place on the eyes. Rest for 10 minutes with the pads in place.*

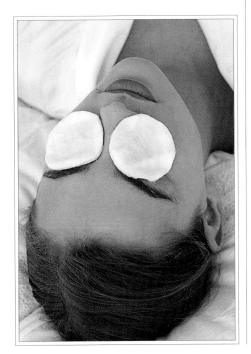

HAYFEVER SYMPTOMS
The membranes lining the nose are most often affected, with either congestion or else a streaming nose and sneezing; frequently the eyes or throat become inflamed too. An all-year-round allergic reaction, or allergic rhinitis, can be set up, with symptoms triggered by mould spores, house dust, fur and car exhaust fumes, for instance.

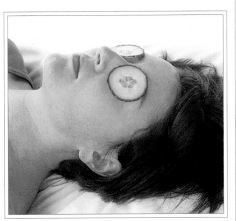

Slices of cucumber may be used on tired, sore eyes in the same way as herb pads.

They can both be used in two ways: firstly, as a tea taken 2 or 3 times a day (in severe cases try an infusion for stronger effect, see page 12) to reduce the inflammation and excess mucus, and, secondly, by soaking pads of cotton wool in a cooled infusion and placing on the eyelids to soothe sore, irritated eyes.

Where the mucus is very watery, alternative internal infusions to the above, or additions to them are:
GROUND IVY (*Glechoma hederacea*): very astringent, reducing excess mucus and drying out the secretions.
RIBWORT (*Plantago lanceolata*): also anti-catarrhal and astringent, toning up and healing the membranes.

HOMEOPATHY

Sometimes it can be worth using Mixed Pollens themselves in homeopathic dilution, before symptoms have started. Otherwise choose from:
ALLIUM CEPA: for a burning nasal discharge; the eyes will run too (think of your reaction to cutting up onions!).
ARSEN ALB: if the eyes are burning, with tears that feel hot. If the nose runs, that too will feel burning, sneezing gives no relief to the irritation.
EUPHRASIA: if the nose runs profusely, with lots of watery mucus, although it may block at night; the eyes feel sore and gritty, with burning tears.

NATUROPATHY

Reduce mucus production by cutting out dairy products (also see Catarrh, page 34), and when the symptoms are severe, take high levels of Vitamin C (up to 2,000 mg per day, unless diarrhoea occurs) to act as a natural anti-histamine.

Rinse out the eyes with an eyebath, using cool distilled water or a proprietary eyewash, to give temporary relief – you can also ease the nose by sniffing up distilled water to wash out the pollens.

INFLUENZA

Anyone who has had influenza will know that it is a more serious complaint than simply having a bad cold. Different viral strains produce differing symptoms, but generally there is a fever, aching muscles, headache and general weakness. Sometimes there may also be a harsh cough. In older, frail people it can seriously debilitate.

AROMATHERAPY

Several oils have considerable anti-viral activity, and help to boost the immune system. It is important though to use them at the earliest sign of influenza for maximum benefit. Either use them in the bath or as steam inhalations (see pages 8 and 33); it may also be a good idea to fumigate the house with oils at the same time, to help prevent everyone else getting the infection. This is best done by either putting 2-3 drops on a radiator to evaporate or else adding around 10 drops to a small plant spray filled with water, frequently spraying the room.

Dried herbs enable you to enjoy herbal teas all year long and are as effective as fresh herbs.

CINNAMON
(Cinnamomum zeylanicum)

Choose from Tea Tree, Eucalyptus, Lemon or Lavender oils.

HERBALISM

In the early stages of a chilled feeling, use a warming tea such as Cinnamon *(Cinnamomum zeylanicum)* – break a stick into a teapot – perhaps with 2.5 ml (½ tsp) of Cayenne *(Capsicum minimum)* or ground Ginger *(Zingiber officinalis)* added. When feeling more feverish, you can provoke sweating by taking infusions (see page 12) of Catmint *(Nepeta cataria)* and/or Elderflower *(Sambucus nigra)*. The deep muscular aching can be relieved by using an infusion of Boneset *(Eupatorium perfoliatum)*, either on its own or mixed with either of the above.

To stimulate the immune system, and also ward off complications such as bronchitis, take plenty of garlic, preferably raw – hot garlic bread or toast is a nice way to take it for all the family.

HOMEOPATHY

Choose from these remedies if not able to get professional treatment:
BRYONIA: if feeling very hot and dry, thirsty for cold drinks, aching all over, headache made worse by movement.

GELSEMIUM: for a hot head and face, but with chills that go up and down the back; burning headache but without any real sense of thirst.
NUX VOMICA: for thoroughly chilled feelings, cannot get warm at all, limbs and back are aching, stomach upset.

NATUROPATHY

At an early stage try having a hot bath to which you add 30–60 ml (2–4 tbsp) of Epsom Salts, then go straight to bed.

Generally restrict the diet, drinking fruit juices until the feverish period has passed, and then starting on fruit, vegetables and whole grains at first. If very hot and sweaty, try applying a cool compress to the chest and trunk.

Immediately the symptoms start, it is advisable to take high levels of Vitamin C to boost the immune system, around 3,000-4,000 mg to start with, reducing over 3-4 days to 500 mg until completely better.

INFLUENZA STRAINS
Influenza occurs in bouts of epidemic proportions, with periodic changes in the viral strains responsible. This makes vaccination programmes more difficult and less effective. Influenza can be a real killer, and attention to good health to prevent the onset of serious symptoms is essential, especially for older people in winter.

LARYNGITIS

Laryngitis is an acute inflammation of the larynx and vocal chords, leading to a very sore throat, hoarseness and even loss of voice. It may follow on from a cold or other infection, or be due to overstraining the voice by shouting, severe coughing or irritations such as smoke or dust.

CAUSTICUM: for a hoarse voice, which may go completely, with a burning, raw throat and irritating cough.

PHOSPHORUS: if you cannot talk louder than a whisper, symptoms may have been brought on by overuse of the voice; with a dry cough and a desire for cold drinks and ice-cream.

NATUROPATHY

Cut out dairy produce to reduce excess catarrh, and take plenty of fruit juices. Try placing a cold compress (see page 15) around the throat, if the problem has been around for a while, it may be an idea to use a hot compress followed by a cold one. Sucking zinc gluconate lozenges not only soothes the throat but directly tackles any infection; in addition to fruit and juices it may be useful to take 500 mg of Vitamin C for a few days, or fresh lemon juice and honey drinks.

AROMATHERAPY

The best method for treatment is undoubtedly steam inhalation (see page 33); the natural choice of oil is probably Benzoin, but you could also use Sandalwood or Thyme. As the oils vaporize with the steam, they soothe the dry, inflamed membranes and ease the breathing as well as being highly antiseptic.

HERBALISM

Local treatment is by gargle; there are a number of useful herbs for this, they are most effective as tinctures (see page 14), otherwise use cooled infusions (see page 12). Choose from these astringent herbs: Sage (*Salvia officinalis*), Thyme (*Thymus vulgaris*), Agrimony (*Agrimonia eupatoria*) or

Holding a towel over your head will concentrate the herbal vapours and delay the effects of evaporation.

Raspberry Leaf (*Rubus idaeus*), which will help to tone up the puffy membranes. For a very soothing effect, add Marshmallow (*Althea officinalis*) to the gargle, or take 10 ml (2 tsp) of a decoction (see page 12) of the root 3 or 4 times a day.

HOMEOPATHY

One of these remedies should be suitable in the short term:

ACONITE: for sudden laryngitis following exposure to cold, dry winds, with a high temperature and a dry cough.

MARSHMALLOW
(*Althea officinalis*)

SINUSITIS

The sinus cavities are air spaces in the bones of the skull, behind, above and below the eyes. They act as a kind of sound-box, helping the voice to resonate. Like the nasal passages they are lined with mucous membranes, and an infection in the nose or throat can spread to the sinuses; acute sinusitis can be very painful and needs prompt treatment. Chronic sinusitis may be linked to allergic reactions such as hay fever.

AROMATHERAPY

Steam inhalations (see page 33) are the best way to work directly on the membranes, loosening thick mucus and fighting infection. Choose from oils of Chamomile, Eucalyptus, Lavender, Peppermint, Pine, Thyme or Tea Tree; a combination may be best, or else change around the oils. In acute sinusitis, the inhalations can be taken 4 times a day to ease the pain and relieve the congestion, reducing to once daily as the symptoms ease, until the sinuses have cleared up.

HERBALISM

Apart from steam inhalations as outlined above, using infusions internally (see page 12) can help to reduce the catarrh and inflammation. Look at the following herbs (see also Catarrh, page 34):

Oil of Eucalyptus is very effective used as part of a steam inhalation.

CATMINT *(Nepeta cataria)*: reduces nasal congestion and helps to liquefy the thick, sticky mucus.

ELDERFLOWER *(Sambucus nigra)*: reduces inflammation by improving circulation through the area, clears long-term catarrh, and eases congestion.

GOLDEN SEAL *(Hydrastis canadensis)*: has an astringent effect, cooling and toning up swollen, inflamed membranes. As this herb is quite expensive and difficult to find loose, it may be easier to take in tablet form, up to 500 mg a day.

It is also often very valuable to take plenty of garlic, either raw or as garlic perles, to fight any infection.

HOMEOPATHY

Try to match the remedy to the symptom pattern – look also at suggestions for Catarrh, Colds or Hay Fever (pages 34, 35 and 39).

CATMINT *(Nepeta cataria)*

HEPAR SULPH: for painful swelling of the nasal cavities, tender to the touch, with infected, yellow mucus discharge.

NAT MUR: a profuse, watery discharge, sneezing and a frontal headache are typical symptoms calling for this remedy.

SILICA: for a dry, blocked nose and a severe headache, perhaps with bouts of sneezing; worse with cold and better with warmth.

NATUROPATHY

Immediately cut out all dairy products, and restrict white flour, pastries, cakes and so on. Eat plenty of fresh fruit and vegetables. Avoid smoky atmospheres, and do not fly when nasal passages are acutely inflamed or blocked, as the changes in air pressure can given severe pain and could damage the eardrum.

Use alternating hot and cold light compresses (see page 15) or just splashes of water around the nose; start with hot water for about 3 minutes and then cold for no more than 1 minute, repeating 2 or 3 times. This will reduce congestion and inflammation, and thus ease the pains. Using an inhalation can be a helpful back-up to this.

SORE THROATS

Sore throats are more and more common nowadays, with increased airborne pollution, smoky, dry atmospheres in air-conditioned buildings and so on. The irritation can range from an annoying tickle to a rasping soreness, and may be linked to other infections. Where the throat inflammation, or pharyngitis, also extends down to the larynx, the voice may be affected – see also Laryngitis and Tonsillitis (pages 41 and 44).

Myrrh *(Commiphora molmol)*

AROMATHERAPY

Use steam inhalations (see page 33) with oils such as Benzoin, Lavender or Thyme. One drop *only* of essential oil of Lemon on 2.5 ml (½ tsp) of honey acts as a powerful local antiseptic, as well as being soothing.

HERBALISM

If possible, use the following herbs as tinctures for gargling; if unavailable then use cooled infusions (see page 12): Agrimony *(Agrimonia eupatoria)*, Sage *(Salvia officinalis)*, and Thyme *(Thymus vulgaris)* are all astringent, toning up the membranes, the latter two also being quite antiseptic. For a more powerful effect try using a tincture (see page 14) of Myrrh *(Commiphora molmol)*, together with one or more of the others. If making infusions, add two broken liquorice sticks to give a more soothing effect, or else use Marshmallow *(Althea officinalis)* leaf in equal amounts with the other herb(s).

HOMEOPATHY

The choice is wide, depending on the causes and the nature of the symptoms. It is advisable to look at other headings in this section too.

APIS MEL: for a red, swollen, burning throat and difficulty in swallowing anything.

KALI BICH: for sharp pains, relieved by swallowing, although there may also be a feeling of a "frog-in-the-throat" which is not relieved. The throat is especially dry and sore first thing in the mornings, with some sticky mucus.

MERC SOL: for a painful and raw throat, with a lot of watery, possibly unpleasant-smelling saliva.

NATUROPATHY

For adults and older children the diet can be restricted to fruit juices only for a day or two at most; younger children and infants will be unlikely to cope with this, so simply reduce the dairy foods and give plenty of fruit juices. If the throat is swollen and feels very hot, try a cold compress (see page 15) around it. If

AGRIMONY
(Agrimonia eupatoria)

OCCUPATIONAL HAZARDS
Many occupations involve excessive use of the voice e.g. teaching, and sore throats are commonplace. The regular use of herbal gargles can ease this discomfort, and help to prevent loss of voice or an actual infection. Keeping the throat moist by drinking liquids often, helps too.

available, suck zinc lozenges. Rest the voice and keep in a warm atmosphere.

In modern offices the dry air leads to frequent sore throats. Sip liquids often, and try to make the air more moist if possible, for example with plants.

Sage *(Salvia officinalis)*

TONSILLITIS

Inflammation and infection of the tonsils most often occurs in children or younger adults; it used to be the fashion to remove the tonsils but unless they become chronically badly infected and act as a focus for other infections, it is now considered better to keep them. They act as an early warning sign of lowered vitality, and if this first line of defence is lost, then more deep-seated conditions can occur in later life.

AROMATHERAPY

Essential oils are not for internal use, unless under qualified treatment, and are rather unpleasant for local treatment. In tonsillitis they are best used as supportive treatment, using steam inhalations (see page 33) of Benzoin, Eucalyptus or Thyme to ease inflammation and fight general infection.

HERBALISM

All the herbs mentioned under Sore Throats (see page 43) for gargling are excellent here too, especially Myrrh (*Commiphora molmol*), Thyme (*Thymus vulgaris*) and Sage (*Salvia officinalis*). For repeated bouts of tonsillitis take garlic daily, either perles/capsules or fresh. Another essential herb to use for chronic

GARLIC (*Allium sativum*)

CONE FLOWER (*Echinacea angustifolia*)

tonsillitis is Cone Flower (*Echinacea angustifolia* or *E. purpurea*); this boosts the immune system and may be taken in tablets or else as a tincture (see page 14), 20 drops twice daily.

HOMEOPATHY

Remedies applicable to tonsillitis include:

ACONITE: for sudden onset of inflammation, with hot, red and burning tonsils and thirst for cold drinks.

HEPAR SULPH: for pain on swallowing, as if something is stuck in the throat, tonsils swollen and discharging a yellow pus.

LYCOPODIUM: for chronic swelling of the tonsils, which look as if they are pitted with small white discharging ulcers; cold drinks make the sensation worse.

NATUROPATHY

The tonsils' actions, in trapping and removing infective bacteria that would otherwise cause deeper problems, means that they are more easily infected themselves. This can produce an infection of the adenoids too, with nasal congestion.

Where these symptoms occur, it is helpful to cut out dairy projects for a while. In any case, take plenty of fluids, especially fruit juices. Freshly-squeezed lemon juice, with a little honey, is a local antiseptic. Repeated attacks of tonsillitis are often a sign of lowered health in general, and may need professional treatment.

THYME (*Thymus vulgaris*)

WHOOPING COUGH

This highly infectious bacterial infection tends to occur in epidemics every few years. Thick, sticky mucus gives rise to a spasmodic cough and the difficulty in inhaling with this gives the characteristic whooping sound. It is mostly seen in children, and in babies it can be serious, so get professional help as soon as possible. Symptoms can linger on for several weeks, so continue to help breathing by the measures listed below.

AROMATHERAPY

Relief for the condition is most dramatic with steam; either use inhalations (see page 33) or with infants simply hold them near steam, such as a basin filled with piping hot water or near a hot bath (make sure they do not touch very hot water). Very good oils to add to the steam are Cypress, Lavender and Tea Tree.

HERBALISM

Start to give herbal teas/infusions at the first sign of coughing – do not wait for the respiratory distress that can set in with the whoop. Use steam to free the mucus, as mentioned above. In young infants and babies, diluted teas

Keep all medicines and aromatherapy oils out of the reach of small children.

should be strong enough; older children may need infusions (see page 12), again diluted (for dosages see page 9). Look at these herbs, and use a blend of the most appropriate:

CHAMOMILE (*Chamomilla recutita*): helps to calm the person down, reduces catarrh and accompanying nausea.
COLTSFOOT (*Tussilago farfara*): one of the best cough remedies, helping to ease the spasmodic nature of the cough.
LAVENDER (*Lavandula vera*): a relaxing expectorant, soothing the cough and breathing and also generally calming.
THYME (*Thymus vulgaris*): highly antiseptic, soothing the dry cough that may herald the start of the problem.
WHITE HOREHOUND (*Marrubium vulgare*): good expectorant, loosening the sticky mucus and reducing spasm.

An alternative treatment that can work wonders is to chop or crush two cloves of garlic into 15 ml (1 tbsp) of honey and leave for a couple of hours, or even overnight. Give up to 5 ml (1 tsp) either neat or diluted in a little warm water, 4 times a day.

HOMEOPATHY

Ideally seek qualified advice for this ailment, but a remedy often used for the characteristic rapid paroxysmal cough is Drosera. Often the bout of coughing can result in vomiting. If children have been in contact with whooping cough, it can be worth trying this remedy as a prophylactic: give 3 doses of 30c dilution (see page 10) in a 24-hour period.

> **SELF-HELP MEASURES**
> Anyone who has heard the distinctive whooping sound will always remember whooping cough. Early treatment is most helpful; self-help measures such as steam treatments can speedily relieve symptoms, but babies and tiny infants should ideally be professionally checked as well.

NATUROPATHY

Keep the fluid intake high, especially if there is vomiting with the coughing bouts; also give only small amounts of light food rather than big meals. Avoid dairy products in order to lessen mucus production, and give easily digested foods.

For older children, supplementing diet with 500 mg Vitamin C daily for a couple of weeks will help to boost the immune system – reduce or stop if diarrhoea develops.

Try to keep the diet light, wholesome and low in dairy foods for quite a while after the initial symptoms have eased, as any build-up in mucus can cause more problems for several weeks.

WHITE HOREHOUND
(*Marrubium vulgare*)

THE CIRCULATORY SYSTEM

Circulation is absolutely vital for health; the blood transports oxygen and all our other nutrients around the body to all the cells, and carries away the waste materials from cellular activity. Without good circulation we simply do not have the fuel to provide enough energy for health. In cooler climates many people suffer from poor circulation, and lowered immune systems can often follow.

Disorders of circulation can occur in the heart or in the blood vessels; the former are not suitable for self-treatment, and for any prolonged or serious circulatory problems it is best to get professional treatment. For example, angina is a cramping of the heart muscles due to narrowing or obstruction of the coronary arteries. When the supply of oxygen to the cardiac muscles does not meet any extra demand, perhaps when walking uphill, the characteristic cramp and pains of angina occur for a short while. Resting eases the pain after a few minutes. Angina can be relieved by taking infusions of Lime Blossom *(Tilia europaea)*, but full professional treatment needs to look at individual causes as well as the health of the heart.

ABOVE: Alternating hot and cold baths is a useful self-help measure for improving circulation. Herbs such as Marigold (Calendula officinalis) *(above left) and Witch Hazel* (Hamamelis virginiana) *can also help astringe and tone swollen veins.*

CHILBLAINS

For people with poor peripheral circulation, living in cool, damp climates often creates chilblains. When circulation is reduced in cold weather, the oxygen supply to the fingers and toes is restricted to the point that the skin cells are damaged and swelling, redness and itching occurs. Warmer weather improves the condition, but using radiant heat, such as warming by the fire, can tend to aggravate the swelling and burning itchy sensation.

AROMATHERAPY

Only use oils locally if the skin is unbroken; otherwise an inflamed reaction may be set off. Massage the affected areas with warming oils such as Black Pepper, Ginger or Marjoram, using a vegetable oil containing a maximum of 3 per cent essential oil. For longer term treatment during the winter months, add oils of Cypress, Juniper, Pine or Rosemary to baths (see page 8 for dilutions), or use them diluted in a base oil as above for regular brisk massage of the hands and feet.

HERBALISM

Locally, use a footbath to which is added a decoction (see page 12) of fresh Ginger root (*Zingiber officinalis*), using up to 15 g (½ oz) per 750 ml (1¼ pt/ 2⅔ cups) of water, or add a tea made from ground Ginger, or for maximum circulatory-stimulating effect Cayenne (*Capsicum minimum*). Do not use the latter if the skin is broken.

Handbaths, or footbaths, are good ways to improve circulation to the extremities. Place hands in a bowl of hot water, with essential oils added as recommended.

GINGER DECOCTION

Ginger can be made into a tea, but a stronger medicine is made from a decoction.

1 Simmer 15 g (½ oz) chopped rhizome in 750ml (1¼ pt/2⅔ cups) water until the liquid is reduced to about 600 ml (1 pt/2½ cups).

2 Strain through a sieve and store in a jug. Give in doses of 5-20 ml (1 tsp -1½ tbsp), three times a day. It will keep in the fridge for 3 days.

Internally, teas from the above herbs will generally improve circulation. For a gentler effect on the extremities use an infusion (see page 12) of Yarrow (*Achillea millefolium*); this dilates the tiny blood vessels in the hands and feet, helping them to warm.

HOMEOPATHY

Since treatment may be needed for a couple of weeks or so, use low potencies such as 6c (see page 10). AGARICUS: if the symptoms are worse when cold, and there is itching and burning with redness of the skin. CALCAREA CARBONICA: if there is relief from cold, the feet in particular feeling damp and cold to the touch. PETROLEUM: if, as well as burning and itching, there is chapping and cracking of the skin; typically the fingers get splits at the tips.

NATUROPATHY

Use alternating hot and cold foot or handbaths, using warm rather than too hot water, for about 4 minutes, and then cold for up to 1 minute. Make sure the feet or hands are well dried. Repeat for 10-15 minutes, nightly for a week if needed. Giving the hands or feet a brisk friction-rub daily will also help the circulation

Increase Vitamin C in the diet by eating more fresh fruit and potatoes; if you suffer badly from chilblains, take a supplement of Vitamin C, up to 1 mg until better, possibly together with 300–400 iu of Vitamin E to improve the elasticity of the blood vessels.

FEVER

The raising of the body temperature, usually in response to an infection, is something that natural medicine sees as generally a positive healing attempt by the body. Most of our vital processes are stimulated by the higher temperature, and conversely many infective organisms cannot survive as well, so the fever response is one that can be aided rather than instantly suppressed.

AROMATHERAPY

In order to encourage sweating at the stage of resolving the fever, a warm bath with a maximum of 10 drops of one of these oils may help – if bathing is not appropriate, use them at 1 per cent dilution in a little vegetable oil and massage the back or chest. Chamomile, Cypress, Lavender or Tea Tree are good choices. For a more cooling effect use 5 drops of oils of Eucalyptus, Lavender or Peppermint in a small bowl of tepid water and sponge the upper back, neck and chest.

HERBALISM

If at the early, shivery stage of an infection, use a tea with Ginger (*Zingiber officinalis*) – 2.5 ml (½ tsp) ground ginger, or peel and grate a small piece of fresh root – and Cinnamon (*Cinnamomum zeylanicum*) – 2.5 ml

CATMINT *(Nepeta cataria)*

CHECKING THE TEMPERATURE

By taking the temperature, and checking on feelings of heat or cold, the stages of the fever can be noted and treatment given. Initially, our internal thermostat is turned up, making us feel cold and shivery; as circulation is boosted and we reach the higher levels, we can feel more comfortable, although with a raised temperature. If the process goes too high, or the infection is not controlled, the thermostat is reset back to normal and we feel feverish and hot. Sweating reduces the temperature. Body temperatures around 38°C (100-101°F) often give the best results in fighting infection. Children's temperatures often go higher, and so may an adult's; if left for too long this can make us feel very unwell and cooling may then be needed, either by inducing sweating or through sponging with tepid water. If in doubt get professional help.

(½ tsp) ground cinnamon, or half a cinnamon stick.

When the fever makes you hot and restless, sweating can be provoked by taking a hot infusion (see page 12) of Elderflower *(Sambucus nigra)*. (At normal temperatures this will not make you sweat.) Other suitable infusions to

ELDERFLOWER *(Sambucus nigra)*

relieve the symptoms are: Boneset *(Eupatorium perfoliatum)*, Catmint *(Nepeta cataria)*, Peppermint *(Mentha piperita)* and Yarrow *(Achillea millefolium)*, while Lime Blossom *(Tilia europaea)* can be added to aid the dilation of the blood vessels and assist general relaxation. Hyssop *(Hyssopus officinalis)* is another excellent herb to calm the system; a tea may be taken frequently while symptoms prevail.

HOMEOPATHY

As with herbalism, there are many homeopathic remedies available and the cause/exact reaction needs to be sorted out first. A few to choose from, in mild feverish states are:

ACONITE: for dry, burning skin and great restlessness and agitation; symptoms may come on quickly.

BELLADONNA: for a high temperature, with a hot, very red face and a racing pulse. In extreme fever cases the person may also be delirious and highly excitable.

EUPATORIUM PERFOLIATUM: for an influenza-type of fever, with chills followed on by heat, aching muscles and maybe sweating.

FERRUM PHOS: for milder fevers, with less obvious causes; a hot, throbbing head and frequent sweating.

NATUROPATHY

Avoid active exercise; take plenty of rest but do not swaddle in heavy bedclothes; keep the room aired.

BONESET
(*Eupatorium perfoliatum*)

Herbs can help combat a fever by either provoking sweating, or by aiding the dilation of the blood vessels.

Drink fruit juices, herb teas or water, and restrict food until the temperature has returned to normal. Sponge the face and chest with tepid water if the temperature is too hot. A cold pack or compress around the trunk will also reduce excessive heat; use something large like a towel wrung out in cold water and wrapped around the body and then wrap in a larger, dry towel or blanket.

Feverish conditions used to be much more common, and traditional practitioners such as herbalists developed quite sophisticated techniques to deal with them. They have become rarer nowadays, but natural measures remain very important in helping to cope with a fever. If the temperature rises to the point where someone becomes delirious or even has a convulsion, get urgent medical aid. Young children can be quite prone to convulsions, but this is rarer as we get older.

HYSSOP
(*Hyssopus officinalis*)

HAEMORRHOIDS

Haemorrhoids, or piles, are swollen veins in the rectum due to a restricted local blood supply and congestion in the pelvic cavity. Occasionally they may protrude externally, and can give rise to bleeding especially with a bowel movement. Piles can occur during pregnancy due to the increased pressure, but are often associated with chronic constipation, when frequent straining to empty the bowels causes extra pressure on the veins.

AROMATHERAPY

Using oils such as Cypress or Juniper in the bath can help to stimulate pelvic circulation; also adding a couple of drops of either to a bowl of cool water and then using this for a compress (see page 15) may help too. Massage of the abdomen (see right) with a 2 per cent dilution of oils of Marjoram or Rosemary can help ease constipation and relieve haemorrhoids.

PILEWORT *(Ranunculus ficaria)*

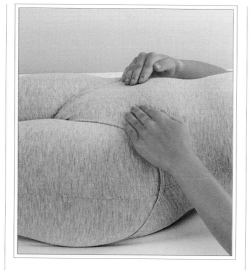

Press fingers steadily into the low abdomen, and massage with small circular movements, to release tension and improve local circulation.

to a small bowl of warm water.

Prolong bleeding from piles can eventually lead to anaemia. Drinking Nettle *(Urtica dioica)* tea may relieve this, but take steps to avoid constipation too.

HOMEOPATHY

Some possible remedies are:
AESCULUS: for a dry itching and stinging sensation, and a tendency for the veins to prolapse and protrude externally.
HAMAMELIS: for a burning soreness, often with bleeding.
SULPHUR: for hot, burning and itching in the anus; the pains are made worse by standing and better when lying.

NATUROPATHY

Practitioners in all of the therapies are likely to give dietary advice, and it is sensible to ensure you eat plenty of fresh vegetables and fruit to give adequate fibre and ease constipation, see also Constipation (page 57). Hot and cold compresses or even hot/cold baths will improve local circulation and reduce congestion; ice packs may be useful to reduce swelling at times. Exercise is also helpful to get the circulation going; ideally get individual advice. Avoid long periods of standing.

WITCH HAZEL *(Hamamelis virginiana)*

HERBALISM

Local treatment can help to astringe and tone the swollen veins. Use commercial creams made with extract of Pilewort *(Ranunculus ficaria)*, Horse Chestnut *(Aesculus hippocastanum)* or Marigold *(Calendula officinalis)*, or use a compress of distilled Witch Hazel *(Hamamelis virginiana)*; the tincture (see page 14) is much more astringent, if available use this diluted at the rate of 15 ml (1 tbsp)

POOR CIRCULATION

Poor circulation to the extremities is quite common in cooler climates, and particularly in elderly people or those who do very little exercise. (See also Chilblains, page 47). Poor circulation can lead on to more serious conditions such as phlebitis or thrombosis, so it should not be neglected, and professional medical help should be sought if in any doubt.

HAND MASSAGE

1 Place some base oil in a bowl, with essential oils added as recommended. Massage into palms of hands with a steady circular movement.

2 Squeeze down the fingers to stretch and loosen them, pushing towards the palm. Repeat steps 1 and 2 several times.

FOOT MASSAGE

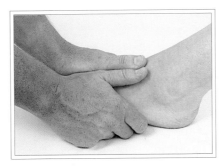

1 To stretch the feet, place hands with thumbs on top of the foot, keeping a firm grip with both of the hands.

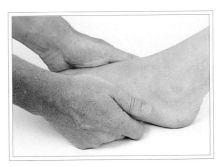

2 Move thumbs outward, as if breaking a piece of bread (be gentle with your partner!); repeat movement several times.

too, and cayenne pepper is the strongest circulatory stimulant, perhaps simply use in cooking for this effect as well as its flavour.

HOMEOPATHY

To improve circulation, the following remedies may be of help in the short term, but if symptoms persist and the fingers and toes become numb, then seek professional medical advice:

SECALE: For cold hands and feet with a burning sensation. The rest of the body also feels cold, and the fingers and

NETTLE
(Urtica dioica)

AROMATHERAPY

Massage the hands or feet with diluted oils such as Black Pepper, Lavender, Marjoram or Rosemary. These can be added to a warm footbath for a stronger short-term treatment. Use a maximum of 10 drops in total, and try a blend of 2 or 3 of these oils. Avoid if skin is broken, get advice first.

HERBALISM

Take hot herbal teas regularly to aid peripheral circulation; choose from Elderflower *(Sambucus nigra)*, Ginger *(Zingiber officinalis)*, Lime Blossom *(Tilia europaea)*, Nettle *(Urtica dioica)* or Yarrow *(Achillea millefolium)*. Daily intake of garlic stimulates blood flow

Exercise is the best way to help yourself in improving circulation. Regular activities stimulate blood flow, and keep the heart and lungs in good condition. Skipping has become more popular as an exercise, and is an excellent way to keep warm.

THE BLOODSTREAM

Since the circulation transports nourishment, both oxygen and nutrients from food, around the body it is essential for our overall health and vitality. Waste matter from all our cells is carried away in the bloodstream for elimination, and white blood cells form an essential part of our immune system. Keeping circulation flowing well, therefore, should be a priority for everyone.

As we get older, circulation tends to slow down and this is exaggerated if we stop exercising or being active. With increasingly sedentary lifestyles in many countries, it is very important to move as much as possible at work, or in retirement, to combat reduced circulation.

toes can become quite blue or white. Take 6c every 30 minutes for up to 10 doses.

CARBO VEG: For cold hands and feet with a mottling of the skin. The skin feels icy cold to the touch and appears blue,

YARROW (*Achillea millefolium*)

CAYENNE (*Capsicum minimum*)

with prominent veins. Skin can also appear blotchy.

NATUROPATHY

Various substances constrict the peripheral blood vessels, most notably caffeine and nicotine, so reducing or cutting out coffee and tobacco will help greatly. Exercise is another essential, wherever possible, and in colder weather keep the wrists and ankles warm as well as the hands and feet themselves. Additional amounts of Vitamin C (up to 500 mg per day) and Vitamin E (up to 400 iu per day) can boost circulation and aid the elasticity of the blood-vessel walls.

CAUTION

Do not increase the doses from those suggested here: it is likely to do more harm than good.

VARICOSE VEINS

Swollen veins most often occur in the lower legs, but can happen elsewhere, see also
Haemorrhoids (page 50). The veins in the legs contain one-way valves that allow blood
to flow back up towards the heart. If the calf muscles weaken, for example after prolonged
standing, or the valves start to work less efficiently from other causes such as pregnancy, obesity
or poor nutrition, then blood collects in the veins, and they swell.

AROMATHERAPY

All the natural therapies are likely to recommend both periods of rest, especially with the feet raised above the level of the thigh to let gravity assist venous return, and exercise to improve muscle tone.

Massage, above the area of varicosed veins and in an upwards direction towards the heart, will reduce the congestion. Essential oils of prime use here are Cypress, Chamomile and perhaps Juniper; use diluted at 2 per cent in vegetable oil.

HERBALISM

Externally, apply tinctures (see page 14) of Marigold (*Calendula officinalis*) or Witch Hazel (*Hamamelis virginiana*), diluted 50:50 with water, 2 or 3 times a day. Internally, a cup daily of an infusion (see page 12) of Lime Blossom (*Tilia europaea*), can help to improve peripheral circulation. Horse Chestnut (*Aesculus hippocastanum*) has a strengthening effect on the blood vessels; it may be taken in tablets as directed, or as the tincture at the rate of 30 drops twice daily.

HOMEOPATHY

CARBO VEG: for a sluggish circulation leading to blueness of the skin, cold extremities and painful varicose veins.

HAMAMELIS: for swollen, congested veins with a purplish blotching under the skin and tired, aching legs; may also have piles.

PULSATILLA: for painful veins, blue in colour; may be associated with pregnancy; pains in legs eased with walking about and in cool, fresh air.

Plenty of fresh fruit is essential in any diet.

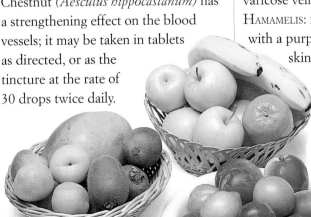

MARIGOLD (*Calendula officinalis*)

NATUROPATHY

Use hot and cold bathing of legs, or spray cool water up the legs at the end of a shower. Walk more; also look at yoga and swimming as good forms of exercise. Reduce alcohol intake; if very overweight try to lose weight steadily.

A supplement of Vitamin E (up to 400 iu daily), together with 5 ml (1 tsp) Lecithin granules daily, can ease the swelling and pains by improving the elasticity of the blood vessels; another helpful substance is Vitamin C (up to 500 mg). In the long term just take plenty of fresh fruit and vegetables and keep fats to a lower level.

THE DIGESTIVE SYSTEM

⊷⊶⊷○⊶⊷

In many respects the digestive system is the most important set of organs in the body, for it is here that we absorb all the nutrients we need in order for all our cells to function and hence for us to survive. The old adage "we are what we eat" has a lot of validity, since poor nutrition can lead not only to problems such as constipation, flatulence or diarrhoea but also to more general ailments like headache, chronic tiredness, poor concentration and memory.

The digestive system is also an integral part of our immune defences, recognizing potentially toxic substances and either breaking them down into safer compounds or else eliminating them. Western dietary and lifestyle habits have created their own disorders, from gastric ulcers to constipation and irritable bowel syndrome; this last condition has become something of a "waste-basket diagnosis" – if nothing else shows up, then that is what you have! Treatment for this should really be individual, as stress, diet, posture and exercise all play a part in each person's symptoms.

ABOVE: Eating fresh fruit is a good way of increasing dietary fibre intake.

ACIDITY AND HEARTBURN

Many people get occasional bouts of acid dyspepsia, usually related to a temporary problem such as having eaten rich, spicy foods or having eaten too quickly when feeling rushed and stressed. If the symptoms happen very regularly, you may need to look more carefully at what you eat and how fast you eat it. If there is persistent discomfort, seek professional treatment; see also Flatulence and Indigestion (pages 59 and 61).

AROMATHERAPY

Using hot or warm compresses (see page 15) over the abdomen, with up to 10 drops of oils such as Chamomile or Lavender in a small bowl of water, can give relief from the inflammation and spasm that accompany excess acidity. These oils, diluted at 2 per cent in a base oil, can also be gently massaged into the abdomen if the discomfort is not too great.

SLIPPERY ELM *(Ulmus fulva)*

HERBALISM

Digestive disturbances generally respond very well indeed to herbal treatment, and acid dyspepsia can be improved considerably. For a temporary problem choose from the suggested herbs and use as warm teas; for repeated acid/heartburn symptoms use stronger, as infusions (see page 12) or as otherwise directed.
CHAMOMILE *(Chamomilla recutita)*: a relaxant and anti-inflammatory remedy that helps the whole digestive tract; if acid symptoms are related to stress and/or over-eating of rich foods, this

HEARTBURN SYMPTOMS
When excess acid leaks back up into the gullet, this inflames and irritates the lining of the oesophagus and the feeling of heartburn is produced. Taking antacid tablets regularly may not only mask underlying problems, but can also be counter-productive as the stomach tries to compensate by creating more acid.

herb makes an excellent choice.
LEMON BALM *(Melissa officinalis)*: another excellent herb where the condition is caused by stress; if available use the fresh leaves for a much finer flavour.
MEADOWSWEET *(Filipendula ulmaria)*: although chemically related to aspirin, Meadowsweet is soothing for an inflamed stomach (but may need to be avoided if there is a hypersensitivity to salicylates such as aspirin) and reduces acidity.
SLIPPERY ELM *(Ulmus fulva)*: this is highly soothing to the inflamed gullet or stomach, and may be taken before meals, either as tablets or by mixing 5 ml (1 tsp) of the pure powder in a little warm water – it lives up to its name as it goes down, coating and soothing the membranes.

HOMEOPATHY

As usual, individual characteristics will determine proper prescribing of remedies, but initially choose from:
CARBO VEG: for a burning feeling in the stomach, and acid reflux with waterbrash (gas being brought up into the mouth with acidic fluid) and sometimes nausea; symptoms often caused by over-eating or drinking.
LYCOPODIUM: for definite heartburn, much wind and a feeling of fullness after only a little food.
NUX VOMICA: when taken too much rich food, alcohol and coffee leading to nausea and acidity but also an empty, hungry feeling in the stomach.

NATUROPATHY

Often a glass of milk is suggested as a temporary measure, to neutralize the acid. This is not always suitable, and certainly not on a regular basis, as dairy produce can create its own digestive problems. It may be helpful to avoid solids for up to 24 hours after a bad bout of acid heartburn. Using a hot compress over the abdomen can relieve pains. Avoid coffee, alcohol, tobacco, chocolate, pastries or spicy foods for at least a couple of days, and if prone to this complaint, then try to slowly cut them out.

MEADOWSWEET *(Filipendula ulmaria)*

COLIC

Colic is the term used to describe spasmodic bouts of cramping pains, especially in the bowel which often associated with trapped gas; see Flatulence (page 59). Colic is especially common in babies. The symptom may be related to tension generally, but if there are other digestive disturbances, do seek professional advice. It is always a sensible precaution to seek medical advice where babies are concerned.

AROMATHERAPY

Gentle massage of the abdomen, in a clockwise direction, using oils of Chamomile, Fennel or Peppermint will help – dilute the oils at the ratio of 3-4 drops per 5 ml (1 tsp) of base oil.

HERBALISM

For an occasional attack of colic, use hot teas of Catmint (*Nepeta cataria*), Chamomile (*Chamomilla recutita*), Fennel (*Foeniculum vulgare*), Ginger (*Zingiber officinalis*) or Peppermint (*Mentha piperita*). Using aromatic seeds like Aniseed (*Pimpinella anisum*), Caraway (*Carum carvi*), Dill (*Anethum graveolens*) or Fennel (*Foeniculum vulgare*) in food, or simply chewing a few of the seeds after a meal can help a lot if you are prone to colic after eating. If the problem is frequent, get professional treatment.

HOMEOPATHY

BRYONIA: if the spasms are made worse by any movement, or by local heat, better by lying still with bent knees.

FENNEL
(*Foeniculum vulgare*)

ABDOMEN MASSAGE

1 Starting in the lower right hand corner, steadily but firmly press in with both hands.

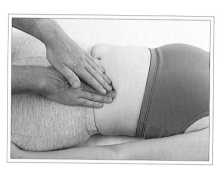

2 Slowly move hands in a clockwise direction around the abdomen, using small circles to massage the colon.

CHAMOMILLA: especially good for colicky babies, or teething infants; the bloated abdomen tends to be improved by local warmth, such as a hot water bottle.

MAGNESIA PHOSPHORICA: if warmth, pressure over the abdomen and walking about ease the discomfort, but burping does not.

NUX VOMICA: for colic brought on by over-eating or drinking alcohol; symptoms eased by sitting or lying down, and worse if upright.

NATUROPATHY

In most cases local warmth over the lower abdomen helps; a hot-water bottle is the easiest method. Internally, herbal teas, as detailed above, will give the best relief, as they not only reduce spasm but aid digestion too. It may well be necessary to look at and treat other digestive problems; see also entries for Constipation, Diarrhoea

ANISEED
(*Pimpinella anisum*)

and Gall-Bladder Problems (pages 57, 58 and 60). If frequent colic occurs, do look at how fast you eat, whether you curl up into a comfortable chair after a meal, or if your diet has a lot of fatty, spicy foods or dairy produce. If any of these apply, try to change that pattern and see if the colic improves without needing other treatment; if not get advice. Often it is most helpful simply to eat meals in a more relaxed way, rather than gulping food down while "on the run".

CONSTIPATION

This is a problem that is largely confined to a typical Western diet and lifestyle. Inadequate amounts of dietary fibre, and perhaps a lack of exercise, lead to the slow passage of faeces through the bowel and this in turn allows water to be re-absorbed, leaving hardened, rabbit-like stools. The frequency of bowel movements is less important than the harder consistency; straining can cause piles (see Haemorrhoids, page 50).

AROMATHERAPY

One of the most effective methods of self-help is daily clockwise massage of the lower abdomen (see page 50), and this can be performed using 2 drops of oils of Lavender, Marjoram or Rosemary in 5 ml (1 tsp) of base oil. Lavender and Marjoram are more relaxing, if tension is a factor, while Rosemary has a more tonic effect.

HERBALISM

Always start with gentle laxatives, or aperients, which increase bowel tone without giving griping. One of the best is Dandelion Root (*Taraxacum officinale*), ideally taken as a decoction (see page 12) – although you may get a gentle action from one of the Dandelion coffee drinks on the market. Another simple herb to use is Liquorice (*Glycyrrhiza glabra*); either chew one of the liquorice sticks that you can buy from a health food shop or add it to the Dandelion Root for the decoction. If constipation persists, switch to trying another herb that works in quite a different way. Linseed (*Linum usitatissimum*) absorbs liquid and creates a soft bulk internally that aids the peristaltic wave movements that propel faeces through the bowel. Take 10 ml (2 tsp) at breakfast, with at least 300 ml (½ pt/1¼ cups) of water. Ideally soak the Linseed overnight in a little water to start the swelling process. It may look like frog-spawn but it can relieve tense constipation! Make sure you take plenty of liquids however.

TYPES OF CONSTIPATION

There are essentially two types of constipation. Where there is inadequate fibre and a sluggish digestive system, treatment should be aimed at toning up the bowel; when the constipation is linked to high levels of stress and spasm, see Colic (page 56), treatment may need to focus on relaxation and even reducing excessive fibre such as bran. If in doubt seek professional treatment, as the regular use of laxatives may be completely counter-productive. Given that approaching $500 million are spent in the United States each year on self-prescribed laxatives, there are good reasons to look at more natural ways!

HOMEOPATHY

As usual, try to match the symptom pattern to the person.
BRYONIA: for hard, dry stools with much thirst and a dry mouth too. The stools can look a very dark brown colour.
NUX VOMICA: for a bloated abdomen; after a bowel movement there is a definite feeling that the bowel has not been properly emptied. Often due to a history of over-eating and chronic use of laxatives.

SULPHUR: for dark, hard stools which are moved only with pain and straining and may cause a burning sensation. Sometimes there is a pattern of alternating constipation and looseness.

NATUROPATHY

In most instances, increase dietary fibre by eating more fresh vegetables and fruit, whole grains and beans or pulses. Bran is a somewhat excessive form of fibre when taken on its own rather than as part of a wholefood meal, so take only small amounts of it, if at all. Ensure that you increase exercise, particularly for the abdominal muscles, and regularly do deeper breathing exercises to encourage the diaphragm to move up and down; this acts internally to massage part of the colon and aid peristalsis.

If constipation occurs after antibiotic treatment, the normal intestinal bacteria can be stimulated by taking a Vitamin B complex supplement, and also with *Lactobacillus acidophilus*. This is the bacteria that turns milk into yoghurt. Taking a little plain, *live* yoghurt daily may do the trick; if this is not enough or if sensitive to dairy foods try one of the proprietary acidophilus supplements.

DANDELION ROOT (*Taraxacum officinale*)

DIARRHOEA

Loose, frequent bowel movements can happen as a short-term reaction to infection, inflammation or food poisoning, and as such are quite a positive, cleansing action. A common experience is holiday diarrhoea, and this is usually a response to exposure to unfamiliar bacteria.

AROMATHERAPY

Massage of the abdomen (see page 56) with antiseptic and relaxing oils like Chamomile, Lavender and Neroli can ease diarrhoea caused by minor upsets and also by anxiety and nervousness. Eucalyptus can be used in the same way if an infection is definitely suspected as the cause. Add Fennel or Ginger if there are griping pains with the diarrhoea. For all these oils, dilute to 3 per cent in a base oil.

HERBALISM

If mild food poisoning or infection has upset the bowels, as well as a choice of infusions (see page 12) listed below, try eating garlic as a natural gut disinfectant.

AGRIMONY (*Agrimonia eupatoria*): astringent and healing to the inflamed and swollen membrane lining the gut, helpful in mild gastro-enteritis.

CHAMOMILE (*Chamomilla recutita*): calming and anti-inflammatory, reduces the impact of tension on the digestive tract. This is one of the first herbs to think of in many digestive disorders.

MEADOWSWEET (*Filipendula*

LAVENDER (*Lavandula angustifolia*)

CAUSES OF DIARRHOEA

Some foods have a laxative effect naturally, for instance prunes or figs, so over-indulgence will give temporary diarrhoea. Stress and anxiety often increase peristalsis and hurry bowel contents through. Repeated diarrhoea may indicate more complex digestive problems and should be treated professionally. Prolonged diarrhoea, especially in young children, can be quite serious as it causes dehydration; ensure adequate fluid intake and seek professional advice. A simple yet dramatically effective rehydration drink can be made by dissolving 5 ml (1 tsp) salt and 15 ml (1 tbsp) sugar in 600 ml (1 pt/ 2 ½ cups) of boiled water. Keep in the refrigerator in a screw-topped bottle and give small amounts frequently. Use for a short time only.

ulmaria): this will help to settle an acidic stomach, see Acidity and Heartburn (page 55), as well as being mildly astringent.

RIBWORT (*Plantago lanceolata*): this has excellent toning, soothing and healing properties for use in diarrhoea from many causes, where there is inflammation.

THYME (*Thymus vulgaris*): this will fight infections and improve digestion generally, settling churning, loose bowels and killing harmful bacteria.

HOMEOPATHY

Many homeopathic remedies feature diarrhoea in their symptom "picture"; three generally useful remedies are:

ARSENICUM ALBUM: typically for diarrhoea from food infected with bacteria; the stools tend to be burning to the skin, dark, greenish brown and smelly.

NUX VOMICA: diarrhoea alternating with constipation, due to over-rich foods, alcohol and so on. Worse after a large meal, any discomfort is relieved by bowel movement.

PULSATILLA: rich, fatty meals, or foods like onions, or excessive nervousness are common triggers for the diarrhoea. The stools are very variable. (Pulsatilla people tend to be gentle, shy, pale and prone to being weepy if ill.)

NATUROPATHY

Try not to use treatments to stem diarrhoea for at least 24 hours, to allow any natural cleansing process to take place. Take plenty of fluids, especially mineral water or herb teas if warm drinks are desired. Moving on to easily assimilated foods such as soups, fruit or vegetable juices helps replace lost nutrients, speeds up recovery and lets the inflamed bowel settle. Plain boiled rice is one of the best first solids, or possibly dry toast.

It may be useful to consider a multi-mineral supplement if diarrhoea was intense, to replenish the minerals lost. Fruit and vegetables can soon be returned to the diet as well.

FLATULENCE

The accumulation of gas in the stomach or intestines can occur as an isolated event, for instance after a meal containing particularly wind-producing foods, or can be a constant, chronic sign of a digestive problem. In the latter case, it may indicate a condition such as diverticulitis or irritable bowel syndrome, and these will need to be addressed in order to sort out the causes of the flatulence.

AROMATHERAPY

Many essential oils have a carminative action, which means that they help to shift gas out of the digestive system (up or down, depending where it is!) and also reduce bloating and spasm that can go with the wind. It may be most appropriate, however, to use the aromatic herbs from which the oils are extracted (see Herbalism entry below). Oils such as Caraway, Chamomile, Fennel, Marjoram and Peppermint could also be used as a warm compress (see page 15) over the abdomen to help relieve the symptoms; use up to 5 drops in a small bowl of warm water.

HERBALISM

A number of herbal teas are excellent at relieving flatulence, but do remember that if this is a major problem to get professional herbal treatment. Choose from Catmint (*Nepeta cataria*), Chamomile (*Chamomilla recutita*), Lemon Balm (*Melissa officinalis*) or Peppermint (*Mentha piperita*) if the problem is in the stomach; any of these plus Dill (*Anethum graveolens*) or Fennel (*Foeniculum vulgare*) if the small intestines seem to be affected, and Ginger (*Zingiber officinalis*) or Peppermint (*Mentha piperita*) for bowel flatulence, although there are several others that may be useful depending on the problem (see other entries in this section).

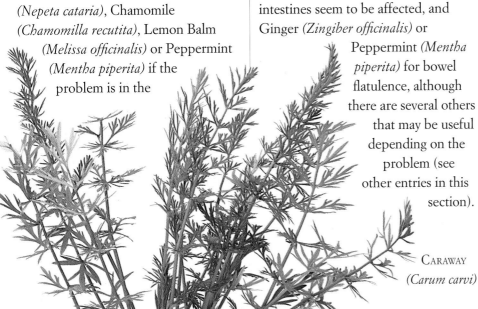

CARAWAY
(*Carum carvi*)

EATING HABITS

A useful starting point for self-treatment of flatulence is to look at eating habits; are you eating very quickly, while tense, or grabbing a bite to eat "on the run"? This is likely to lead to swallowing gas with the food; inadequate digestive enzymes may be produced and the meal can ferment in the intestines rather than be properly digested.

This leads to more gas being created and flatulence gets worse. Also, take care not to do a lot of bending, or sitting curled up on a low sofa, immediately after a meal, as this encourages a gas build-up with bloating and collicky pains.

HOMEOPATHY

Several remedies featured elsewhere in this section may help; try to look beyond the flatulence to deeper causes and seek the remedy for those. Initially, pick from Chamomilla, Carbo veg, Nux vomica or Pulsatilla, for flatulence brought on by eating too rich or too big a meal.

NATUROPATHY

Often flatulence can be caused by eating too heavy a mixture of foods – consider reducing the fat content of your diet, and restricting the combinations of proteins and carbohydrates you eat. If this helps a lot, then you might want to consider exploring the Hay system of eating (see Reading Suggestions, page 125, for further sources of information).

One reason for flatulence can be after administration of antibiotics, as the intestinal bacteria have been decimated; these can be encouraged to multiply by taking plain "live" yoghurt, or possibly more concentrated supplements such as *acidophilus* tablets/powders. A high-fibre, raw-food diet is often recommended for general health; this is in itself likely to give you more gas, especially if you switch over suddenly to this kind of diet. The increase in bacteria needed to cope with the fibre creates a lot of wind. Some flatulence is therefore quite natural, if not exactly sociable! It is often better to change the diet more gradually to ease the problem.

GALL-BLADDER PROBLEMS

Gallstones may steadily grow in size or number with very few symptoms for a long time, except perhaps increased indigestion or flatulence, but may cause acute colic if the gall-bladder gets inflamed. Gallstones need professional treatment, and sometimes surgery, but there is much that can be done to ease the discomfort alongside qualified medical help.

AROMATHERAPY

Not really a first-choice discipline, but warm compresses (see page 15) over the right side of the abdomen, using diluted oils of Lavender, Marjoram or Rosemary, may relieve spasm and colic.

HERBALISM

Start with the most gentle herbs. If gallstones are definitely present, a scan is needed to establish their size before any treatment is prescribed. CHAMOMILE (*Chamomilla recutita*) tea is both anti-inflammatory and anti-spasmodic, and gently stimulates the whole digestive process.
DANDELION ROOT (*Taraxacum officinale*) is an excellent mild liver tonic; ideally

Marjoram (Origanum majorana)

make a decoction (see page 12) and take a small cupful twice a day. Look also at the herbs listed for Colic and for Flatulence (pages 56 and 59); they are

---

DANDELION DECOCTION
Although dandelion leaves can be made into a tea, a stronger medicine can be made from the roots by making a decoction.

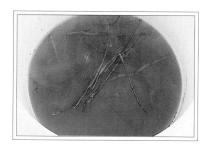

1 Simmer 50 g (2 oz) clean, chopped root in water.

2 Strain through a sieve and store in the fridge. Give in doses of 5-20 ml (1 tsp-1½ tbsp), 3 times a day. It will keep for 3 days.

ROSEMARY (*Rosmarinus officinalis*)

likely in most cases to aid digestion and relieve congestion in the liver and gall-bladder.

HOMEOPATHY

As a short-term measure, try a few doses of either of these before consulting a qualified practitioner:
BRYONIA: where food lies heavily in the stomach, there may be nausea, biliousness and headache.
NUX VOMICA: for feelings of nausea in the mornings, if brought on by rich meals.

NATUROPATHY

Disturbances in the gall-bladder, with or without gallstones, will affect how well fats are digested, so the first step is to restrict animal fats and dairy produce, while increasing vegetables and fruit. To encourage bile production and flow, eat vegetables such as artichokes and bitter salads such as endive and chicory, as well as taking plenty of garlic and fruit to reduce cholesterol (lemon juice is powerful in this respect). Use smaller amounts of light oils such as Olive, Sunflower and Safflower in dressings.

INDIGESTION

Indigestion is a general term for discomfort, often accompanied by bloating, acidity, heartburn, nausea or bowel disturbances (see other entries in this section). Usually it is a temporary problem, brought about by eating too much or the wrong kind of food, excess alcohol or from stress. Longer-term digestive pains may be caused among other reasons by taking aspirin-related drugs, by heavy smoking or other digestive ailments.

AROMATHERAPY

A warm compress (see page 15) including Chamomile or Lavender oils may give some relief, or try gently massaging a 2 per cent dilution of one of them into the abdomen if indigestion is milder.

HERBALISM

Herbal teas in the first place may well sort out the immediate indigestion, choose from:
CHAMOMILE (*Chamomilla recutita*): for the effects of over-eating, also if in a stressed state.
LEMON BALM (*Melissa officinalis*): for nervous indigestion; related to meals or not, settles a churning stomach.
MEADOWSWEET (*Filipendula ulmaria*): for acid indigestion, especially if accompanied by some looseness in the bowels.

LEMON BALM (*Melissa officinalis*)

PEPPERMINT (*Mentha piperita*)

PEPPERMINT (*Mentha piperita*): for indigestion with plenty of flatulence and bloated abdomen, or even nausea. Also think of taking Slippery Elm (*Ulmus fulva*) if indigestion pains are persistent, either 5 ml (1 tsp) of the powder blended in a cupful of water, or the pure tablets, with one or more meals, to soothe the stomach.

HOMEOPATHY

For an occasional bout of indigestion, try a couple of doses (see page 10) of:
ARGENT NIT: where there is a lot of wind, with belching and possibly heartburn, a craving for sweet or fatty foods which tend to upset the digestion and give diarrhoea.
LYCOPODIUM: for pains and wind; if hungry but can only take small amounts of food, worse with cold foods or drink.
NUX VOMICA: useful for the effects of eating and drinking too much, causing pain, heartburn and even vomiting.

NATUROPATHY

If indigestion is quite bad, cut out solid food for 24 hours if possible, taking only herb teas or fruit juices (particularly pineapple which contains digestive enzymes), and reintroduce foods gently, starting with something light like soup or puréed apple. If indigestion is repetitive, try taking a Vitamin B complex supplement as a digestive stimulant, or else look at a digestive enzyme supplement such as Pepsin in the short term, but it may be better to get professional treatment. Avoid drinking lots of fluid at mealtimes, as this will dilute your natural digestive juices.

Chamomile tea is a relaxing aid to the digestive system.

MOUTH ULCERS

These small ulcers, that can occur on the tongue, gums or the lining of the mouth, are sometimes due to local trauma, for instance biting your cheek or wearing ill-fitting dentures, but often they reflect a state of generally being run-down. Recurrent "crops" of mouth ulcers may therefore need more overall treatment; see Stress (pages 28-9) as well as anything directed locally.

AROMATHERAPY

The essential oil of choice for treating mouth ulcers is undoubtedly Myrrh. This is not only astringent and healing but also has an anti-fungal property; one of the reasons for mouth ulcers can be fungal infection, for example *Candida albicans* (the cause of thrush). Myrrh is best used in tincture form (see Herbalism below); you can make your own in small amounts by dissolving the essential oil in alcohol – use 5 drops in 5 ml (1 tsp) of a spirit such as vodka or brandy. This can be applied neat right on to the ulcers, or use 2.5 ml (½ tsp) in a little water as a mouthwash. You can add 1 drop of oil of Fennel to make it taste better, dissolving it thoroughly.

HERBALISM

Local treatment is by means of herbal tinctures (see page 14), to stimulate healing

CONE FLOWER
(*Echinacea angustifolia*)

and reduce the inflammation. The strongest, although worst tasting, is Myrrh (*Commiphora molmol*); others to choose from are Marigold (*Calendula officinalis*), Sage (*Salvia officinalis*) and Thyme (*Thymus vulgaris*). Pay attention to general health, and seek professional treatment if the ulcers are persistent or recurring. Cone Flower (*Echinacea angustifolia* or *E. purpurea*) may be a useful herb to take; it boosts the immune system and is widely obtainable in tablet form, or a tincture of the fresh plant is also available – take 10 drops in water 3 times a day.

HOMEOPATHY

Remedies are more likely to be of benefit if they are chosen for the background causes, but some examples of those remedies that are of value for the ulcers are:

BORAX: for painful small ulcers that feel hot in the mouth and may even bleed, when eating for instance.

MERC SOL: when there is an unpleasant, metallic taste in the mouth, with larger, almost greyish ulcers and perhaps bleeding gums; good for oral thrush.

NAT SULPH: for very painfully sensitive ulcers which may look like blisters, the discomfort is relieved by something cold such as an ice cube.

NATUROPATHY

Recurrent mouth ulcers can often indicate a poor diet, or nutritional deficiencies. Nutrients most likely to be

MYRRH (*Commiphora molmol*)

lacking, and consequently of most benefit in treating the problem, are Vitamin B2, Vitamin C and zinc, and supplements of these may be needed in the short term until the diet can be improved to give sufficient amounts – increase green leafy vegetables, fresh fruit, whole grain bread (including the wheatgerm) and for non-vegetarians eat some meat and fish.

Mouth ulcers most often occur at times of stress or when the immune system is lowered in some way, so it is generally advisable to look at ways of reducing the impact of stress (see pages 28-9) if ulcers are recurring frequently.

For direct local treatment, try applying pure wheatgerm oil, for example by piercing a natural, oil-based Vitamin E capsule, and dabbing a little on to the ulcer. If there are foods, for instance vinegar, that do aggravate the ulcers, obviously leave them out of the diet for a while.

NAUSEA AND VOMITING

There are a great many reasons for feelings of nausea, or actual vomiting. Often this is a temporary reaction, for example to over-eating or drinking, food poisoning, a gastric infection, violent coughing, travel sickness, or associated with a migraine; if nausea or vomiting is persistent, then professional help is essential. Children in particular can easily become dehydrated from repeatedly vomiting.

AROMATHERAPY

Warm compresses (see page 15) over the stomach may be of help. Choose from oils of Chamomile, Lavender or Peppermint, up to 5 drops in a small bowl of water. Taking 1 drop *only* of oil of Cloves or Peppermint, on a sugar lump, may help to directly settle the stomach. A useful oil to spray around the sick room is Lemon, this is not only helpful to allay feelings of nausea but also is much fresher smelling and less sickly than some oils, so will be generally appreciated by the household!

HERBALISM

The remedy of first choice is probably Ginger (*Zingiber officinalis*); either take frequent sips of a weak tea, or of 10 drops of tincture (see page14) in a little water, or chew a small

CAUSES OF NAUSEA

Nausea or vomiting can usually be linked to a specific situation – eating too much rich food, or drinking too much alcohol, anxiety or travel are common triggers. Continual feelings of nausea indicate a greater disturbance; again this may be obvious as in morning sickness of pregnancy. Where the cause is not obvious, and if symptoms are not quickly cleared up with self-help, get medical advice as soon as possible.

CRYSTALLIZED GINGER

piece of fresh ginger. Another possibility – say, for travel sickness – is to chew a little crystallized ginger, or drink flat ginger ale.

Other potentially useful herbs to settle the stomach are Chamomile (*Chamomilla recutita*), Lemon Balm (*Melissa officinalis*) and Peppermint (*Mentha piperita*); try weakish herb teas. All these herbs aid digestion generally, and ease flatulence, so can help to sort out the causes of nausea as well as the symptoms themselves.

HOMEOPATHY

As ever, try to establish the causes and the overall pattern. In the meantime, useful remedies include:
ARSENICUM ALBUM: for severe nausea, perhaps associated with diarrhoea, and a great thirst but unable to take more than a few sips at a time.
IPECACUANHA: for sudden and persistent nausea or vomiting, with much watery saliva and frequent belching; symptoms are made worse by cold drinks.
NUX VOMICA: following over-indulgence or excessive drinking, nausea may come on soon after the meal, with waterbrash and food coming back into the mouth.

NATUROPATHY

Obviously keep off solids in the short term, but do keep up fluid intake, either warm or cool drinks depending on preference. When the sickness has subsided, re-introduce light, easily assimilated foods such as clear soup, then slightly more solid dishes like plain whole grain toast, boiled brown rice and cooked vegetables. Gradually return to your normal diet over a couple of days. Smaller meals will be helpful. If anxiety is producing the nausea, then relaxation exercises will help; see Anxiety and Stress (pages 19 and 28-9).

LEMON BALM
(*Melissa officinalis*)

The Reproductive System

The health of our reproductive system is completely intertwined with our general health. Our creative and reproductive energies derive from our basic vitality, and it is this that herbalism seeks to sustain and enhance. With self-treatment, therefore, it is also sensible to look at overall health. Many books, for instance, link together the reproductive and urinary systems; clearly they have physical links, and treatment for conditions such as an enlarged prostate will affect urine flow directly.

Tension and stress can strongly disturb hormone production, and conversely during hormonal changes, such as the menopause, there is a lowered capacity to cope with stresses. Good nutrition, exercise and posture all affect our reproductive organs. It thus makes sense to give yourself a general overhaul if you have any of the problems discussed below, and do remember that the suggestions made are no substitute for professional treatment.

A word of caution for women who are pregnant or intending to become pregnant. The following aromatherapy oils should be avoided during pregnancy (particularly during the first five months) because of their strong diuretic properties or tendency to induce menstruation: Bay, Basil, Clary Sage, Comfrey, Fennel, Hyssop, Juniper, Marjoram, Melissa, Myrrh, Rosemary, Thyme and Sage. Use all essential oils in half the usual quantity during pregnancy and take extra care when handling them. Ensure that the oils you are using are pure essential oils, as adulterated blends or synthetic oils can sometimes have less predictable effects. Because of their potentially toxic nature and strong abortive qualities, Oreganum, Pennyroyal, St John's Wort, Tansy and Wormwood should only be used by a qualified aromatherapist and must be avoided during pregnancy.

RIGHT: A healthy diet, with plenty of whole grain foods, is essential to all our body systems.

IMPOTENCE

The inability of a man to achieve or maintain an erection is a condition that most often results from mental or emotional problems, perhaps anxiety in general or about a particular relationship or sexual situation. The whole area of sex drive is a major subject in its own right (see Reading Suggestions, page 125); there are often physical causes of persistent infertility, but libido can be improved in many ways.

AROMATHERAPY

Due to the subtle yet profound impact that aromatic essential oils can have on our moods and emotions, they can play a very positive part in reducing the effects of stress on libido. One obvious way to use them is in the bath; another may be to get your partner to give you a massage with diluted essential oils (2.5 per cent dilution in a carrier oil), this should be with the aim of creating close contact without the pressure of needing to "perform" – if making love does result that's fine, just don't make it a condition of the massage!

Suitable oils to consider include Sandalwood (which is often liked by men as well as women), Jasmine, Neroli and Ylang Ylang. These are all likely to have a relaxing and uplifting effect. One factor in choosing an oil is because you like the smell; this may seem desirable generally but in this kind of problem it is obviously essential.

HERBALISM

As outlined in the introductory section, the herbal approach should be to look at boosting vitality and better health. Many herbs that may help with problems of impotence are thus tonics; they may have other actions over time, and so only use the suggested herbs for a short period, say 3 weeks, before taking a break or seeking professional advice.

Where tension is a major factor, try using Oatstraw (*Avena sativa*) in tablets

DAMIANA *(Turnera diffusa)*

or up to 2.5 ml (½ tsp) of the tincture (see page 14) twice daily. If exhaustion or depression are more significant, then take teas of either Damiana *(Turnera diffusa)* or Rosemary *(Rosmarinus officinalis)*: these are both tonics and Damiana in particular is valuable in toning the male hormonal system. Another possibility is Ginseng, which helps our systems adapt better to excess stress. This is available in tablet or liquid form – there are really three kinds, with varying effects: Asiatic *(Panax schinseng)* which is more stimulating, American *(P. quinque-folium)* which is more relaxing, and Siberian *(Eleutherococcus senticosus)* which is an unrelated plant with similar tonic properties.

Ginseng remedies should generally be avoided by people with very high blood pressure, without first seeking professional herbal advice.

HOMEOPATHY

Undoubtedly the best results will be found by seeing a professional homeopath, since there are so many factors which will determine the best remedy. Some examples are:

ARGENT NIT: a good remedy where there is a lot of apprehension or fear, in this case about a relationship or sexual situation.

KALI PHOS: strengthens the nervous system, when exhaustion or even depression is interfering with general vitality. Good for younger people, who have temporarily exhausted themselves.

SEPIA: for loss of sex drive and lowered interest in your partner and the relationship. Good for slightly older people, or those more chronically run-down, tired and exhausted.

NATUROPATHY

Sexual vitality depends on general health and well-being, and so attention should be paid to diet. Of particular benefit are Vitamins E, B and C, and also zinc (10 mg), and there may be a case in the short term for supplements of these, possibly in a multi-vitamin and mineral tablet.

Exercise, and also adequate rest, are both important, and splashing warm and cold water around the pelvic area will stimulate circulation. For similar reasons, avoid excessively hot baths before intercourse. Finally, don't drink a lot of alcohol as a means of trying to reduce anxiety before intercourse – it doesn't help in maintaining an erection!

MENOPAUSAL PROBLEMS

The change of life, when periods cease, can be a tremendously variable experience; for some women there is very little disturbance to their lives, except for the relief of no longer having monthly bleeding. For others, symptoms such as hot flushes, anxiety, insomnia, heavy periods, depression or severe vaginal dryness make their lives thoroughly miserable for a long time. Each person is different; don't hesitate to get advice.

AROMATHERAPY

During the pre- or peri-menopausal phase, which may last for years leading up to the point when ovulation finally stops, the periods may become quite erratic (see also Menstrual Problems, page 68). Useful oils to think of include Geranium and Rose, both of which seem to have a regulating, balancing effect on the female hormone cycle. Also, uplifting oils such as Bergamot, Neroli or Jasmine can help a great deal with the emotional swings that may occur – other life changes, such as children growing up and leaving home for the first time can often

ROSE *(Rosa species)*

HORMONE REPLACEMENT THERAPY

Conventional treatment has now focused on hormone replacement therapy (HRT), and while this has helped ease the symptoms for a lot of women, others react badly to it and it is very clearly not suitable for everybody. There are other ways of helping the process, some of which are described below.

coincide at this time, so there may be a general sense of upheaval and loss.

For all these oils, either use a few drops in the bath, or dilute to 1 per cent in a base oil and massage into the skin. Try ringing the changes with the oils too, so that you do not use one exclusively for more than a couple of weeks. While it may not seem scientific, if you are drawn towards the scent of a particular essential oil, then it is most often what you need at the time!

HERBALISM

Many herbs have quite powerful hormonal effects – the contraceptive pill itself was originally derived from a species of Mexican Yam – and professional treatment may be needed here. A common herb which can often improve problems such as hot sweats, depression and irritability, is Sage *(Salvia officinalis)*. Not only is this a tonic for the nervous system, and reduces excess sweating, but it has oestrogenic activity and can ease the dramatic drop in hormone levels that upset the whole system. Take 2 small cupfuls of an infusion (see page 12) for a month to see if it is helping.

Another herb with hormonal effects is Chaste Tree *(Vitex agnus castus)*. The berries are used, and act via the pituitary gland to encourage the ovaries, and seem to have a more progesterogenic effect (see also Pre-menstrual Symptoms, page 71). This herb may be taken as a tea or in tablet form (up to 300 mg per day); do not overdo the dosage as this can induce an itching sensation on the skin, and as always if there is no improvement, then seek professional advice. Simple relaxants like Chamomile *(Chamomilla*

Chaste Tree
(*Vitex agnus castus*)

recutita) and Lime Blossom (*Tilia europaea*) may help to reduce some of the emotional swings that may happen during the menopause.

HOMEOPATHY

The emphasis of all these therapies is to assist the normal changes that occur with the stopping of menstruation, without trying to interfere to any great extent. Homeopathic treatments will similarly aim to encourage the physiological and mental adjustments. On a self-help basis, you may find some relief from excessive symptoms with remedies such as the following:

HRT and Heart Disease

Recent information has suggested that HRT may be helpful in protecting against some kinds of heart disease; this does, however, need to be balanced against an increased risk of some other diseases. An active lifestyle on the other hand can provide good health benefits for the heart and circulation, as well as the bones and muscles, and should be thought of as an essential part of good health during and after the menopause.

PULSATILLA: for hot flushes with a lot of sweating, perhaps giving a musty odour. If cold drinks generally ease symptoms, then this may be a suitable remedy.

SEPIA: for sudden hot flushes, with a feeling of faintness, reddened face and probably some sweating. Warmth may actually help to ease the discomfort. May be inclined towards anxiety or irritability.

NATUROPATHY

Keeping to a healthy diet can do wonders for overall vitality, and this in turn helps to give you greater resilience against any problems during

the menopause. Hot flushes may be eased by taking additional Vitamin E, around 100 iu twice a day, while at least 500 mg calcium per day, preferably in a supplement containing a little Vitamin A and D and magnesium, can help to prevent osteoporosis from calcium loss. It is essential to continue to do some exercise, such as walking, cycling or even jogging, which also helps to maintain calcium levels as well as strengthening the heart and lungs.

LIME BLOSSOM (*Tilia europaea*) *is a simple relaxant which may help reduce the emotional swings which are often associated with the menopause.*

MENSTRUAL PROBLEMS

Disturbances in the menstrual cycle can be of various kinds, and can be due to a wide number of factors, so it is essential to take a broad, holistic view of health. For persistent problems, or if self-help does not correct matters, do seek professional help.

AROMATHERAPY

In order to get relief from painful periods, with cramping pains, a gentle and slow abdominal massage may be needed. Using oils which aid relaxation of muscle spasm, such as Chamomile, Lavender, Lemon Balm or Marjoram, will help a great deal. If massage cannot be tolerated, try using a few drops of one of these oils in a hot compress over the abdomen. Lemon Balm, often called Melissa oil after its Latin name, also has a generally balancing effect on the menstrual cycle; however, it is highly concentrated, and very expensive (often adulterated) and drinking a tea from the fresh leaves may be more suitable for longer term treatment. Rose oil seems to have regulating effects too, but is also expensive.

Many essential oils have a stimulating effect on the uterine muscles, and need to be avoided in pregnancy, or suspected pregnancy – used as above, they may be useful in scanty or irregular bleeding. Refer to the list on page 64 for a list of oils to avoid in pregnancy, but avoid all essential oils if in doubt that pregnancy is a possible cause and get professional advice and treatment.

HERBALISM

Menstrual disorders are an area where herbal medicine comes into its own for two reasons: firstly, many herbs have quite significant hormonal effects and, secondly, the holistic

TYPES OF MENSTRUAL PROBLEMS

Lack of periods altogether (or amenorrhoea) can happen due to emotional traumas, excessive exercise, sharp swings in weight such as loss brought on by anorexia or physical debility; irregular periods may result from similar causes, and of course both disturbances can happen when going into the menopause. More commonly for many women, periods may become too painful (dysmenorrhoea) – this may be due to a hormonal imbalance (see also Pre-menstrual Symptoms, pages 71-2). Excessively heavy menstrual bleeding (or menorrhagia) may happen without any obvious cause, but can also indicate more complex disorders such as fibroids or pelvic infection. A potential problem with menorrhagia is the risk of becoming anaemic. Finally, don't forget one of the most obvious reasons for lack of periods – pregnancy!

approach of herbalism means treatment can help restore overall balance much better than simply using synthetic hormones.

Painful periods may be relieved in the first place by taking infusions (see page 12) of either Lemon Balm (*Melissa officinalis*) or Chamomile (*Chamomilla recutita*). More severe cramping can be eased with a decoction (see page 12) of either Cramp Bark (European Cranberry Bush) (*Viburnum opulus*) or Valerian (*Valeriana officinalis*) – both of these taste quite disgusting, so may be better in tablet form (up to 5 g).

Heavy periods may be regulated by infusions of Yarrow (*Achillea millefolium*) or more strongly by Lady's Mantle (*Alchemilla vulgaris*) or White Deadnettle (*Lamium album*) – these are also all useful to drink to reduce leucorrhea, or discharge, between periods; if anaemia is suspected, try drinking ordinary Nettle tea regularly. Some herbal remedies are perhaps best left to professional practice, especially when hormonal imbalances are behind the symptoms.

HOMEOPATHY

The need for professional help in complex cases also applies to homeopathic treatment, but here are a few possible remedies for occasional problems:

ACONITE: for suppressed menstruation due to a sudden shock or from getting

VALERIAN (*Valeriana officinalis*)

LADY'S MANTLE
(*Alchemilla vulgaris*)

thoroughly chilled
(getting cold feet,
literally or
metaphorically).
NAT MUR: for irregular
periods, which may be
profuse when they
do start; associated
with feelings of
general sadness and
when possibly the delay is
due to emotional upset.
PULSATILLA: for painful, spasmodic and
scanty periods most often linked to
tension; can be helpful when periods
have failed to start in puberty.

NATUROPATHY

Exercise is beneficial in improving
blood flow through the pelvic
basin. During a period this may speed
up the bleeding but will also
probably shorten the length of
the bleeding, and reduce
muscle spasm. Hot
and cold
applications to the
lower abdomen and
back will have similar
effects – these can be
done by finishing a
shower by reducing the
temperature for a few
seconds, or by
splashing with
cool water at

the end of a
bath, or even
using hot/cold
compresses (see page
15). A diet high in natural
fibre from vegetables, fruit,
pulses, beans and whole
grains will not only
provide nourishment for the
reproductive system but will also help
to avoid constipation which can
accompany painful periods.

Useful supplements may include
calcium, preferably with magnesium,
to ease painful cramps if taken just
prior to and during the period
(around 500 mg). Vitamin E, up
to 300 iu daily, may be useful
during this time of the cycle
too, especially if periods are scanty and
painful. Both iron and folic acid may be
required if there is any sign of anaemia.

*Regular exercise improves pelvic
circulation and muscle tone, thereby
reducing congestion and cramps.*

SELF-HELP MEASURES
A major factor for many women in
producing disturbances of the
menstrual cycle is excessive stress.
This can cause irregular, scanty or
painful periods for instance.
Changes in lifestyle, to include
more opportunities for relaxation,
perhaps increased exercise and an
improved diet, can have a dramatic
effect on hormone levels and
menstrual patterns.
Another potential cause of irregular
periods is sudden and drastic
dieting. Excessive dieting is never a
good idea, and can result in the
temporary loss of periods
altogether. If you need to lose
weight, do it gradually and under
the guidance of a professional
dietician or your family doctor.
Natural forms of medicine and
treatment may be required
alongside self-help, but don't
neglect the latter.

Oil of Evening Primrose, or a
similar supplement such as
Starflower oil, may be
valuable in helping to
regulate the periods.
Evening Primrose oil may
be taken just for 10 days
pre-period, up to 2,000
mg, or throughout
the month at half
the dosage.

MORNING SICKNESS

At least half of all pregnant women experience nausea or vomiting during the first 12 weeks or so of their pregnancy; only in rare circumstances does this become so severe as to warrant drugs or hospital treatment. There seems to be good reason to link the sickness, which may actually occur at any time of day or night, with a lowered blood sugar level, and it is often very useful to eat regularly to maintain a more even state.

AROMATHERAPY

Essential oils can be of some use in this condition – their concentration and powerful effects, however, mean that caution is needed during pregnancy with all oils (see page 64 for further advice). For nausea, simply try smelling a drop of Ginger or Peppermint oil on a paper tissue.

HERBALISM

The prime remedy for nausea, including morning sickness, is Ginger (*Zingiber officinalis*). This can be taken in various ways; try chewing a piece of crystallized ginger, or even a piece of peeled fresh ginger, or making ginger tea and sipping frequently. A very useful method is to eat biscuits (cookies) made with fresh ginger, nibbling one as and when the need arises – this temporarily raises the body's sugar level as well as providing the effect of the ginger itself. Other useful herbs are Chamomile (*Chamomilla recutita*) and Peppermint (*Mentha piperita*) taken as teas; as a practitioner I have found that in pregnancy the smell of the former often seems to be more off-putting than any benefit from the herb, but see for yourself.

> **CAUTION**
> While the suggestions made here are all well-tried and safe, it is not advisable to self-treat during pregnancy. This book is <u>not</u> a substitute for seeking professional or medical advice, this is especially true for ailments during pregnancy.

HOMEOPATHY

There are several remedies in which nausea or vomiting are major indications; try one of these for a few days to see if they give any relief:

IPECACUANHA: for continual nausea, and frequent vomiting, which does not give much relief. The tongue generally seems quite clean in appearance.

NUX VOMICA: for nausea and a lot of retching; it may be more difficult to vomit but it does help ease the nausea. The tongue is coated and may look almost brown.

SEPIA: mostly just for nausea, especially associated with smelling food or getting chilled; or

PEPPERMINT (*Mentha piperita*)

GINGER (*Zingiber officinalis*)

when the symptom is relieved with warm drinks or possibly a warm application to the stomach.

NATUROPATHY

The fact that early morning is a particularly bad time for getting the nausea confirms the importance of the blood-sugar levels; try keeping some whole grain biscuits by the bed to nibble if you feel empty and nauseous on waking. In general avoid greasy or fatty foods and cut down on coffee and alcohol. A diet with plenty of whole grains, pulses and vegetables will help to keep blood-sugar levels more constant, as will eating at regular times during the day.

Eating a piece of fruit when hungry can help keep nausea at bay.

PRE-MENSTRUAL SYMPTOMS

There are a number of symptoms that can occur in the second half of the menstrual cycle, i.e. leading up to the period, due mostly to imbalances in hormone production. These symptoms tend to be lumped together by the medical profession into pre-menstrual syndrome (PMS), but not all women experience them in the same combination or in the same way.

AROMATHERAPY

Essential oils can be helpful in reducing fluid retention; this is most effectively done by using them with lymphatic drainage massage, so do see a professional aromatherapist if this is a major part of your symptoms. Using oils such as Geranium, Grapefruit, Juniper or Rosemary in the bath, and also doing skin-brushing, frequently stroking your limbs up from the extremities towards the heart, are good methods of self-help.

HERBALISM

Probably the most valuable herb for disturbances of the second half of the menstrual cycle is Chaste Tree (*Vitex agnus castus*). The berries are used, and they help to normalize

COMMON **PMS** SYMPTOMS

Symptoms include mood changes, with irritability and/or weepiness, headaches and sometimes migraines, fluid retention, tender breasts, and deep aching in the low abdomen or thighs before and at the start of the period. This half of the cycle can also be when creativity and energy, including sexual energy, can be higher so do not automatically assume that the pre-period phase has to be awful.

hormone function, particularly in lifting progesterone levels – lowered progesterone is most often the trigger for the symptoms. They can be

COUCH GRASS
(*Agropyron repens*)

obtained in tablet form. In very large amounts Chaste Tree can give an irritating sensation under the skin; if this occurs simply stop taking it.

Herbs which have diuretic effects may be useful in giving some relief; try infusions (see page 12) of either Cleavers (*Galium aparine*) or Couch Grass (*Agropyron repens*) – yes, this scourge of gardeners does have important medicinal properties! Two other helpful herbs are Chamomile (*Chamomilla recutita*), both as a diuretic and gentle relaxant, and Lemon Balm (*Melissa officinalis*) which eases the emotional

SKIN BRUSHING

1 To improve lymph drainage in the legs and thighs, try daily skin brushing. Lightly and briskly brush the upper legs in an upwards direction a few times, from the knees to the thighs.

2 Then brush the lower legs upwards a few times. Repeat steps 1 and 2, always starting with the upper leg and always brushing upwards towards the heart.

LEMON BALM
(*Melissa officinalis*)

swings that may happen. In recent times one herb that has gained a high reputation for balancing hormonal swings is Evening Primrose (*Oenothera biennis*), and it may be worth taking capsules of this in the second half of the period cycle, between 1,000 and 2,000 mg are usually needed. Any improvement in symptoms may take 3-6 months to appear.

HOMEOPATHY

Some possible remedies are:
CALC CARB: for overweight people who feel the cold easily if only during this phase, and have clammy hands and feet; may also experience tension and low abdominal pains.
CALC PHOS: for cold but drier extremities, pains and cramping, with pre-menstrual bloating.

Women for whom either of the above remedies are suited will probably get relief from pre-menstrual discomfort by taking a warm bath or using a hot-water bottle.
LYCOPODIUM: this may be appropriate when there is a good deal of pre-period irritability and tension, which quickly ease when the period starts. Abdominal

STRESS AND PMS

It can be easy to label all physical and emotional upsets as PMS (men tend to this very often), and overlook other causes of problems. Try to keep a check on whether symptoms definitely occur in monthly cycles. A good way of doing this is to keep a diary to keep a record of mood swings and general discomfort. Tension and irritability can be due to over-stress, or genuine relationship problems, which need to be sorted out. Trying to relax can also help if in a stressful situation (see also Stress, pages 28-9).

pain associated with this tension is the major physical symptom.

NATUROPATHY

Both diet and exercise can help tremendously in minimizing pre-menstrual problems. Cut down on alcohol and coffee during this part of the cycle at least, as they both affect fluid balance, and drink plenty of water to encourage kidney

EVENING PRIMROSE
(*Oenothera biennis*)

function. There has been a lot of evidence that Vitamin B6 can reduce symptoms; this is probably best taken as a supplement (up to 50 mg) as part of a whole Vitamin B complex, maybe with the addition of magnesium (200 mg). Evening Primrose oil has already been discussed earlier; for both this and Vitamin B6 it may be easier to take half the suggested doses throughout the whole of the month.

Regular exercise such as walking, cycling, swimming and running can help reduce the pelvic congestion that may accompany PMS; similarly, splashing hot and cold water around the lower abdomen regularly will improve circulation (see also Menstrual Problems, pages 68-9).

CAUTION

Never mix herbal remedies with homeopathic ones. You should always keep to one system, rather than swapping between the two. Do not increase the dosages suggested here – herbs and plants are very powerful and can produce adverse effects if used without due care and attention. If in any doubt, consult professional advice.

PROSTATE PROBLEMS

The prostate gland is situated at the base of the bladder, and produces part of the seminal fluid. It surrounds the urethra, but normally causes no problems for urine flow. It is roughly the size of a walnut, but a common condition as men get older is a benign enlargement. This leads the prostate to compress the urethra, and perhaps even the bladder, and urine flow becomes slower to start and/or stop, with some dribbling.

AROMATHERAPY

To be used only as an adjunct to seeking professional treatment. Where there is benign prostate enlargement causing some difficulty in passing urine, placing a hot compress (see page 15) using a few drops of oils of Chamomile, Juniper or Pine over the low abdomen can quickly ease the pressure and get the urine to flow better. If the prostate is inflamed, oil of Chamomile should be included due to its anti-inflammatory effect.

HERBALISM

For an enlarged prostate, an infusion (see page 12) of one or both of the following remedies can help a good deal:

HORSETAIL (*Equisetum arvense*): a strong

SCOTS PINE (*Pinus sylvestris*)

INFLAMMATION OF THE PROSTRATE

Another problem can be prostatitis, or inflammation of the prostate, possibly due to a low-grade infection, and this can produce frequent, uncomfortable urination and tenderness of the gland itself. More rarely, although important to bear in mind in older men, prostate cancer can occur. This is, of course, outside the scope of self-treatment; it may be symptomless for some time, until the swollen gland restricts urine flow.

diuretic, increasing urine flow and helping the bladder to empty itself completely – failure to do so can lead to cystitis. It is also astringent and anti-inflammatory, toning the swollen membranes.

WHITE DEADNETTLE (*Lamium album*): another astringent remedy, which seems to have a regulatory effect on blood flow through the pelvic area, and so can reduce excess swelling of the prostate.

These two herbs combined can soothe the membranes and improve urine flow.

Benign prostate enlargement is often associated with lowered testosterone levels, and Saw Palmetto (*Serenoa serrulata*) is a very useful herb in this context. The berries not only have a diuretic and urinary antiseptic effect, but they also have a hormonal action to address the underlying problem. A decoction (see page 12) is strongest, but the berries could be taken with one or both the other suggested herbs in infusion form.

HOMEOPATHY

Some possible remedies are:

APIS MEL: when there is inflammation, probably with some enlargement, so that there is a frequent desire to pass water, but with only small amounts of stinging, burning urine.

BELLADONNA: when urination is also painful and difficult; the pressure causes some involuntary dribbling of urine when standing or moving around.

PULSATILLA: for frequent, urgent need to pass water, slight dribbling, or incontinence with any movement such as coughing, laughing or sneezing.

NATUROPATHY

Stick to a varied wholefood diet, with plenty of fluids during the day to keep urine moving through the bladder, but reduce coffee, tea or alcohol which can all irritate. Zinc is of special benefit to the prostate. Pumpkin seeds are a good food source and a supplement (up to 20 mg) may be needed daily for a while if symptoms of enlarged prostate develop.

Hydrotherapy treatment is a valuable aid; use alternating hot and cold water for the low abdomen (3 minutes hot and maximum 1 minute cold), either using a shower or splashes in the bath. The ideal method is using Sitz baths, as in hydrotherapy spa clinics.

THRUSH

Thrush is the common name for a fungal infection of the mucous membranes by the yeast *Candida albicans*. It can affect the mouth, and this is sometimes seen in tiny babies, or around the anus or on the penis, but most commonly it is a vaginal infection. A number of things can trigger off an attack of thrush; one of the major causes is often a course of antibiotics, which seriously destroy our helpful, defensive bacteria.

AROMATHERAPY

One of the most significant natural anti-fungal agents is essential oil of Tea Tree. This is available in pessary (insertable) form in some countries, but the oil can be used in the bath or in more concentrated form in a hand-basin of water; use 6 drops in warm water and bathe the vaginal area with it. Although Tea Tree oil is much more soothing than most anti-fungal drugs, do use it well diluted at first in case of any irritation. Other useful oils to use in this way are Lavender and Myrrh, and they could be blended with Tea Tree to help speed up healing.

HERBALISM

Herbalists will probably give much of the advice discussed under Naturopathy below, and are equally likely to recommend the above oils for local use; other herbs that have healing, soothing and anti-fungal effects include Marigold (*Calendula officinalis*) and Cone Flower (*Echinacea angustifolia* or *E. purpurea*). These are best used in tincture form (see page 14); dilute at the rate of 5 ml (1 tsp) to 600 ml

LAVENDER (*Lavandula angustifolia*)

OTHER POSSIBLE CAUSES OF THRUSH

Quite often a vicious circle can be set up by an infection: cystitis – treated by antibiotics – leading to thrush. Other factors can be the contraceptive pill, frequent digestive infections, a diet high in sugars, or generally being over-stressed and run-down. Conventional treatment involves the use of anti-fungal creams, or pessaries; both of these treatments may be irritating to the membranes, and self-help measures can often be the best route to avoid repetition of the infection.

(1 pt/2½ cups) of warm water, and use as a local wash. For oral thrush in babies apply a little with a cotton bud (swab), and in adults use 5 ml (1 tsp) of the tincture in a little water as a mouthwash. A powerful internal anti-fungal remedy is garlic, and if thrush recurs frequently, taking either fresh garlic or garlic capsules daily can help to combat general yeast infection. It can also be used locally, although it may irritate the vaginal

membranes if they are very inflamed – peel a clove of garlic, dip it in olive oil (you may want to tie a piece of cotton thread around it, so you don't lose it inside!), insert in the vagina and leave overnight.

HOMEOPATHY

Treatment will focus on internal remedies, backed up by local self-help measures (see next page). Practitioners may even prescribe homeopathic doses of *Candida* itself, but some other possible remedies are:
MERC SOL: for reddish patches, especially if oral thrush when there may be blisters on the mucous membranes, with thick, slimy discharge and some mould-like odour.

NAT MUR: for white spots, less of a discharge but more painful irritation; in oral thrush

CONE FLOWER
(*Echinacea angustifolia*)

MARIGOLD
(*Calendula officinalis*)

there may be painful blisters on the lips or tongue. Drier and more inflamed symptoms make this more suitable as a remedy than Merc sol. SULPHUR: for an itching and burning sensation, and a thick, white discharge with some odour. In oral thrush, Sulphur may be indicated when there is a foul taste and odour, lots of white blisters or yeast coating in the mouth, and dry, rough lips.

NATUROPATHY

Fungal infections thrive in warm, damp environments, so it is important to keep the vaginal area cool and dry, and let it "breathe" more freely – only use cotton underwear, and avoid tights or tight jeans. Do not use bubble baths or strong vaginal deodorants as they can disturb your normal defences. Apart from the oils or herbs to use locally, you may find it helpful to wash with salt water – use about a handful of salt in a hand-basin of warm water. If you are in an active sexual relationship, it is important for both of you to look at these suggestions, as you may re-infect each other without joint treatments. Live, natural (plain) yoghurt can also be used locally, on a sanitary towel (napkin) or tampon; this helps to encourage the defensive bacteria to multiply. If a recent course of antibiotics seem to be the cause, then eating live yoghurt will aid the defensive flora in the gut too.

Since yeasts will flourish on sugars, reduce all concentrated sugar and refined carbohydrates in the diet, and also severely restrict alcohol. Eat plenty of vegetables and whole grains, and use a fair amount of olive oil for any salad dressings, as this has a natural anti-fungal effect (it may be applied sparingly locally too, especially if the area is dry and inflamed). As a supplement, *Lactobacillus acidophilus* has a significant effect on suppressing yeast invasion and encouraging the gut flora; it is the bacteria which converts milk into yoghurt, but occurs in much higher concentrations in the capsules or powder that are quite widely available. If diarrhoea develops, then stop taking it immediately.

A diet high in fresh vegetables, and low in refined sugars, helps to prevent recurrent thrush.

Pure Olive oil, as used in salads, has a natural anti-fungal effect.

THE URINARY SYSTEM

Our general health and vitality are often mirrored in the health of our urinary system. If we are chronically stressed or run-down, we are much more likely to be prone to recurrent cystitis or other urinary infections. Conversely, disorders of our kidneys have a weakening effect on our energy overall, and need to be treated by professional practitioners.

The urinary system is essential in maintaining the fluid balance within the body, and together with the heart and circulatory system it controls blood pressure. Equally importantly the kidneys keep our electrolytes, or fluid-soluble minerals, in balance and aid in removing toxins. Problems of urination can arise not only from infection or serious illness, but are affected by hormonal changes and in men the functioning of the prostate (see The Reproductive System, page 64), and by stress. Muscle tone is also important, especially as people get older and the bladder tends to shrink, or atrophy, and exercises can be helpful for maintaining control of bladder function.

ABOVE: Dandelion (Taraxacum officinale) is a highly effective diuretic. It is also rich in potassium, thereby counteracting any loss of potassium that occurs through urination.

CYSTITIS

Cystitis is an acute infection of the bladder, which may often recur and become a chronic condition. It is more common in girls and women than in boys or men, due to the much shorter length of the urethra in women; in many women it can be triggered off by irritation during sexual intercourse, and useful advice can include emptying the bladder before sex (if pre-meditated enough!) and certainly afterwards.

AROMATHERAPY

Essential oils have quite powerful antiseptic properties, and should be used at the earliest possible stage of cystitis. A useful way to use them is to add them to the bath, up to 10 drops in total added just before getting into the water. Some of the most suitable oils are Bergamot, Chamomile, Lemon (perhaps only use 5 drops if this oil is chosen), and Sandalwood. A warm compress (see page 15), with 3-5 drops of Chamomile or Lavender oils added, can be placed over the lower abdomen if there is a lot of discomfort.

HERBALISM

There are many herbs which have specific effects on the urinary tract, so if the cystitis persists or recurs, do seek professional treatment. In the first instance, drink plenty of fluid,

BEARBERRY *(Arctostaphylos uva-ursi)*

CYSTITIS SYMPTOMS

Symptoms of cystitis can include frequent urging to pass water, accompanied generally by a sharp pain – in women this is usually felt in the urethra, and there is usually inflammation (urethritis) here too, while men tend to experience pain in the penis. The urine may look cloudy or strongly coloured and may have a strong smell. Sometimes there is pain just before or just after urination, perhaps with a feeling of needing to pass water again as fresh urine trickles into the inflamed and irritated bladder.

---

especially water or infusions (see page 12) chosen from the following herbs. In mild cases simply drinking plenty of herb teas such as Chamomile *(Chamomilla recutita),* or Meadowsweet *(Filipendula ulmaria)* may reduce the inflammation sufficiently to solve the problem. These two herbs can of course also be taken as stronger infusions in acute attacks. Buchu *(Barosma betulina)* is a particularly useful herb, not only acting as a urinary antiseptic but soothing the inflamed

BUCHU *(Barosma betulina)*

membranes too, and helping to escape the cycle of cystitis-antibiotics-cystitis which can easily occur with conventional treatment. Bearberry *(Arctostaphylos uva-ursi)* is another strong antiseptic remedy, most helpful when the urine is acidic and sharply burning. To these herbs can be added Celery Seed *(Apium graveolens)*, which has a very alkaline effect on the urine, Agrimony *(Agrimonia eupatoria)* to tone and astringe the swollen tissues, and/or Marshmallow *(Althea officinalis)* (ideally the root, but the leaf is also good) for its pure soothing properties. It is generally recommended to take plenty of garlic internally to fight infection and to cleanse the tissues for some time after the attack has subsided.

HOMEOPATHY

Symptoms of discomfort when passing urine are a feature of the "remedy picture" (see Introduction to

MAKING BARLEY WATER

Home-made lemon barley water is a nutritious drink to take in place of tea and coffee when suffering from cystitis.

1 Cover 100 g (4 oz) of pearl barley in a little water and bring to the boil, strain and throw away this water. Pour 600 ml (1 pt/2½ cups) of boiling water over the barley (or ideally simmer the barley in 750 ml (1¼ pt/3⅔ cups) of water for 5 minutes, to extract the full benefit.)

2 Add the zest of a lemon and leave to cool. Strain and keep the liquid in the fridge. Drink often.

Homeopathy, page 10) for a large number of homeopathic medicines, so the professional practitioner has a wide choice. For self-treatment, choose initially from:

CANTHARIS: for the classical symptoms of cystitis, burning pains with passing water, which comes only slowly, and also a frequent urge to urinate.

PULSATILLA: for a great urge, and urgency to urinate, causing some pains and distress. Urine may easily dribble out, when coughing or laughing.

STAPHYSAGRIA: when the vulval area is sore or bruised – often given for "honeymoon cystitis".

NATUROPATHY

In the first place, as soon as you feel the twinges of cystitis coming on, drink plenty of water, or herb teas. Avoid alcohol, or strong tea and coffee, which can irritate the bladder lining further. Sometimes it can be helpful to add a pinch of bicarbonate of soda to water to make it alkaline. Avoid obviously acidic foods such as vinegar, unripe fruit or ones like gooseberries, plums, rhubarb or tomatoes.

Many people tend to suffer periodically with cystitis, and for recurrent problems, look at things such as not wearing tight jeans or trousers, avoid vaginal deodorants and be careful to rinse underwear thoroughly (biological washing powders or detergents can leave irritant traces). If you have had antibiotics, it is very helpful to take plenty of live yoghurt afterwards to repopulate the defensive gut bacteria; a little can also be applied to the vaginal and urethral openings for local effect, especially if you are prone to cystitis.

This helps to alter the local acidity, which encourages the body's natural defences to multiply, and it is also quite cool and soothing to the irritated and inflamed surface.

FLUID RETENTION

Excess fluid in the tissues, or oedema, can happen in a variety of ways. Local, temporary swelling will occur with an injury, for instance a sprained ankle or a large bruise (see First Aid, page 104, for treatment). Fluid retention in the thighs and hips in women is often associated with a build-up of toxins, as in cellulite, and a general detoxifying programme of diet, exercise and massage will be most effective.

AROMATHERAPY

For problems such as fluid retention linked to cellulite, or temporary ankle swelling due to heat or long flights, massage the legs and thighs in an upwards sweeping movement, with a 1-2 per cent dilution of essential oils in a base oil (see page 17). Beneficial oils are Geranium, Grapefruit, Lemon and Rosemary; Juniper has an even stronger diuretic effect, stimulating the kidneys to excrete excess fluid, but do not use if there is any

FENNEL
(*Foeniculum vulgare*)

OTHER CAUSES OF FLUID RETENTION

Fluid retention is often aggravated during the pre-period phase (see also Pre-Menstrual Problems, page 71), especially in the breasts and abdomen. In hot weather most people find that they have some fluid retention, and ankles tend to swell during long plane flights – drink plenty of fluid (but *not* alcohol), and move about the plane as much as possible.

Severe leg and ankle oedema is often a sign of kidney and/or heart malfunction, and should be treated professionally, without delay, as should any unexplained or prolonged fluid retention.

kidney problem or in pregnancy. Another essential oil of value is Fennel, but this has a mild oestrogenic action too, so be careful not to use for long if oedema is hormone-related.

Pregnancy is a time when ankles might swell, but use essential oils sparingly (less than 1 per cent), if at all, and get professional advice if you are unsure. Do not use Fennel or Juniper, and only use Rosemary later on, from the fifth month of the pregnancy, if ankle oedema is a problem.

HERBALISM

In order to encourage the removal of fluid, the simplest approach is to use herb teas which have a diuretic effect. Do not use for more than a week at a time; long-term stimulation of the

THIGH AND LEG MASSAGE

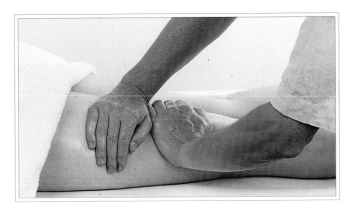

1 To improve circulation in the legs, firstly oil the legs. Place hands on the thigh and stroke upwards to the buttock a few times, with light but steady sweeping movements, hand-over-hand.

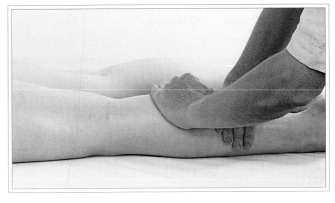

2 Move hands down to the lower leg and stroke up to the back of the knee a few times. Repeat steps 1 and 2; always start this movement on the upper leg, and always stroke up towards the heart.

urinary system can be tiring and if the swelling has not subsided within a short period, qualified advice and treatment may be necessary.

One of the best herbal diuretics is Dandelion Leaf (*Taraxacum officinale*), indeed its common name in many languages translates as "Wet-the-bed"! When you pass urine, potassium is lost in the fluid, and with some prescribed diuretics this can lead to a potassium deficiency, which is itself a serious condition. Dandelions are so rich in potassium that this loss is

Dandelion leaves can make a strongly diuretic tea.

counteracted. Make a tea and drink three cupfuls a day initially.

Other common and useful herbs are Chamomile (*Chamomilla recutita*), Fennel (*Foeniculum vulgare*) (but see Aromatherapy section earlier), Meadowsweet (*Filipendula ulmaria*) and Yarrow (*Achillea millefolium*), all of which are diuretic among their other properties.

For just increasing the amount of urine passed, without strain on the kidneys, the best herb is the creeping rhizome of Couch Grass (*Agropyron repens*). In the short term this can be taken as a decoction (see page 12).

HOMEOPATHY

Because of the complexity of the causes of fluid retention, and the fact that homeopathic remedies are aimed at the person's constitutional make-up as far as possible, it is much better to seek professional homeopathic treatment for any water retention. For purely first aid problems such as bruising causing some local swelling, see First Aid, page 104.

NATUROPATHY

Since fluid retention in the ankles and legs is often associated with circulatory problems like

YARROW (*Achillea millefolium*)

varicose veins, all the general advice given under that section (see page 53) will be useful. Exercise is vital to improve the blood flow, and hence speed up the removal of fluid. Look at the diet, and in particular at salt intake; in most cases it will be very beneficial to reduce salt intake, since excessive amounts of sodium encourage fluid retention and also place an undue burden on the kidneys.

Massage is most helpful, especially gentle lymph drainage techniques – for self-massage, lightly and repeatedly stroke the affected areas in movements directed towards the heart. If the swelling is in the legs for instance, stroke the upper legs first in an upwards direction, before repeating the action to the lower legs, so that the fluid has somewhere to drain into from the ankles.

Try to have the legs raised, supported on something soft such as a cushion, to allow gravity to assist in draining fluid back towards the heart. In a similar way, swelling of the wrist can be eased by raising the arm or supporting it in a sling. Continued swelling, in any part of the body, requires medical attention.

URINARY INCONTINENCE

The inability to control the bladder and prevent dribbling of urine, or bed-wetting, is something that can affect people at both ends of life in particular. Children may get into problems with involuntary bed-wetting through something simple such as a chill or shock, or from a deeper upsetting worry, or just because they sleep too deeply (see Children's Ailments, page 112).

AROMATHERAPY

Alongside any self-help measures such as pelvic floor exercises, an excellent essential oil to use is Cypress, which is astringent, toning up the tissues and encouraging efficient excretion of fluid. Use it in the bath, about 6 drops, or make a compress with 2 drops in a small bowl of warm water and wring out a small towel in the liquid, placing it over the low abdomen. For daily use it may be easier to use a diluted oil, 2 per cent dilution (about 50 drops in 100 ml (3½ fl oz/½ cup) of base oil), and massage a little into the lower abdomen each day. Another oil that may help in this way is Pine, but use 1 per cent of this only. In either case do not use daily for more than 10 days at a time.

HERBALISM

Probably the foremost herb for this condition is Horsetail (*Equisetum arvense*), which is quite a strong diuretic, but more significantly it contains appreciable amounts of silica. This has an astringent and toning effect on the bladder tissues, encouraging it to empty efficiently and regain some of the lost muscle tone. Horsetail is perhaps best taken as the fresh juice, available in some countries, take 10 ml (2 tsp) twice a day; otherwise a decoction may be taken (see page 12). If emotional upset is a part of the problem, then also taking St John's Wort (*Hypericum perforatum*) may help a good deal – use the juice at the same rate or take an

HORSETAIL (*Equisetum arvense*)

infusion (see page 12) for a week or two (take care not to overdo this remedy if going out in strong sunlight, as it can increase sun sensitivity). For individualized treatment get professional help.

HOMEOPATHY

Several possibilities exist within homeopathy for treating this condition, some suggestions with a brief "snapshot" of the symptom picture for each remedy are:

ARGENT NIT: with incontinence at night in particular, although also possible in the day, brought on by nervousness, restlessness and anxiety. This remedy is useful for older people who may easily get anxious, perhaps over a move or travelling, and hence become incontinent; the urine may burn a little when passed.

BELLADONNA: with a constant urge to pass water when awake; there may be some involuntary dribbling when

standing, and also during sleep.

PULSATILLA: this remedy is often appropriate for shy, sensitive people who are prone to crying. It is helpful if they experience bed-wetting at night, whether children or older people; there may be an easy tendency to dribble in the daytime too, with difficulty in retaining urine.

NATUROPATHY

One of the first things to look at is the muscle tone within the pelvic basin generally. Exercises such as alternately tightening and relaxing the buttocks can help to regain control of the bladder and urethra. Another exercise that may be useful is to try and stop in midstream while actually urinating, and hold for a couple of seconds before restarting to pass water. If done regularly, this can be a great aid in tightening and strengthening the muscles of the bladder.

Another approach is to employ hot and cold water applications to the lower abdomen and back. This can be via alternating hot/cold compresses, around 3-4 minutes hot and 1 minute cold, repeated once or twice. A simpler method is to have a fairly warm bath, followed by a short splash of cool water around the waist and bladder, or else when finishing a shower turn the temperature down to cool and use on this area for a minute. These methods will help to stimulate pelvic circulation. which in turn will encourage better muscular control.

THE MUSCULO-SKELETAL SYSTEM

P roblems of the muscular and/or skeletal systems are for most of us simply a fact of life, ranging from simple aches and pains after unaccustomed exercise or effort, to the inevitable wear and tear on our bodies as we get older. In the great majority of cases these problems represent "everything that we don't die of", yet their impact on our health, vitality and mobility can be enormous, causing great problems. Back pain alone is the major cause of time lost from work in most industrialized countries, and the often crippling discomfort of chronic arthritis reduces the quality of life for sufferers by a considerable amount.

While it is true that wear and tear are a part of living, their effects *can* be lessened and much greater levels of comfort and mobility are possible. It is perhaps a sobering thought that much of our predisposition to problems with skeletal disorders in later life is established in the first few years of childhood; prevention, especially in terms of diet, is an important part of the equation therefore, and very hard to achieve when adult. Changes to lifestyle later on can make differences however, together with some of the suggestions under the sections that follow.

ABOVE: Massaging with aromatherapy oils is a wonderful and natural way to ease the body.

ARTHRITIS

Although specialists identify up to 200 divisions of arthritic conditions, it is useful to think of arthritis falling into two categories: osteoarthritis (OA) and rheumatoid arthritis (RA). Osteoarthritis is the natural wear and tear of the joints that occurs with ageing, as the cartilage surrounding the bones becomes thinner and the surface becomes rougher. This leads to friction and degeneration occurs as the joint gets deformed.

AROMATHERAPY

The two principles of many natural approaches to arthritis, namely detoxification and improving circulation around the joints, are the main aims of aromatherapy treatment. Essential oils which aid tissue cleansing include Cypress, Juniper and Lemon, and these can be used as bath oils (see page 8) regularly. Juniper also has an anti-inflammatory and mildly analgesic effect; similar properties are found in Chamomile, Lavender and Rosemary oils. These may all be used either in the bath or diluted in a base oil and gently massaged into the affected areas. If this is painful or difficult to do, they may be used in a hot compress (see page 15); try combining any two of these oils for greater effect, varying them to avoid overuse of any one oil. To stimulate the circulation, use oils such as Black Pepper, Ginger, Marjoram and

Rosemary in any of the above ways. As you can see, some oils have overlapping effects and can help with relieving arthritic discomfort in many ways.

HERBALISM

The herbal pharmacopoeia are full of herbs that can be of benefit in treating arthritis; as mentioned above, it is useful to think of treatments in terms of detoxifying and stimulating the circulation, thus removing the need for local inflammation, as much as any simply pain-relieving action. For self-help treatment, apart from the dietary advice discussed below, an initial cleansing programme can be adopted. In order to remove acidic toxins, make a tea from Celery Seed (*Apium graveolens*), which has an alkaline effect on the whole system. Use just 5 ml (1 tsp) of the seed, perhaps lightly crushing the seeds with the back of a spoon before making the tea.

Another herb which increases elimination, via the urine, is Parsley (*Petroselinum crispum*); add 5 ml (1 tsp) of the chopped fresh herb to the above tea for maximum effect. Two cups of this tea daily for a week or two can have considerable benefits.

To improve the circulation you need

A warm compress on the affected area can help relax muscles.

OTHER CAUSES OF ARTHRITIS

Other factors include previous injuries and occupations – high amounts of some sports, or physical jobs such as farming can lead to greater wear on certain joints. Since it is sometimes associated with an excess of acid waste matter in the body accumulating around the joints, diet is important too.

RHEUMATOID ARTHRITIS

Rheumatoid arthritis is a different problem altogether. It is an inflammatory process that seems to be what is called an auto-immune disorder, meaning the body's defences for some unknown reason start to attack its own cells. In RA, not only are the synovial membranes lining the joints inflamed and thickened, but the bone underneath is steadily destroyed, leading to painful and often badly deformed joints. People are quite likely to feel ill in themselves as a result of this disorder, and professional treatment is essential to try to deal with the underlying condition.

look no further than Ginger (*Zingiber officinalis*); chop up a small piece and make a tea from it, or add to the mixture above. For a more direct anti-inflammatory action, a couple of suggestions are Meadowsweet

(*Filipendula ulmaria*) and Feverfew (*Chrysanthemum parthenium*). An infusion (see page 12) of Meadowsweet may be taken twice daily, while Feverfew may be taken in tablet form. The fresh leaves of Feverfew can also be chewed and eaten instead; just three leaves a day is a medicinal dose, but occasionally they can give mouth ulcers.

HOMEOPATHY

As a first treatment of arthritis, try one of these remedies:

BRYONIA: this is applicable for hot joints, when the pains are worse with warmth or with movements, and seem to be eased by the use of cold applications or compresses (see page 15).

PULSATILLA: if the pains and inflammation seem to move rapidly from one joint to another, with a quick change in symptoms. A pulsatilla-type of person usually feels much better in the fresh air, and this remedy seems to suit women better.

RHUS TOX: this is often the first remedy to be thought of in many rheumatic conditions; symptoms are better with warmth and after some movement, while the person is likely to feel stiff and painful after some time of resting. Cold, damp weather also makes the symptoms worse.

NATUROPATHY

Attention to the diet is an important part of treatment, and ideally this should be adapted individually by a practitioner. In most instances, it is essential to eat plenty of fresh vegetables, raw or cooked, and also fresh fruit – although citrus fruits are often to be avoided by sufferers. Other foods to reduce include red meats, cheeses, sugary foods and excessive coffee or tea. An approach that

Place 5 ml (1 tsp) of lightly crushed celery seeds in a teapot. Pour on boiling water and leave for 5 minutes to infuse. Sprinkle 5 ml (1 tsp) chopped fresh parsley on top of the tea, strain and drink a cupful.

PASQUE FLOWER (*Pulsatilla vulgaris*)

has found some popularity is the Hay diet, named after its originator Dr Hay. The diet essentially involves avoiding combinations of proteins and carbo-hydrates at any one meal; this is beyond the scope of this section, but has been written about in other books.

To relieve stiffness, especially in winter in cooler, less sunny climates, there is a lot of value in taking cod liver oil capsules, one or two a day. The occasional use of a bath containing Epsom salts is also excellent to ease stiffness and discomfort; dissolve 60 ml (4 tbsp) of the salts in a hot bath and soak for 15 minutes. In an acute inflammatory stage of arthritis, with very hot joints, try using an ice-pack or cold compress. Often in chronic conditions, with cold, stiff joints, a warm compress is better (see page 15).

CRAMP

Acute and very painful contractions of muscles produce the feelings of cramp. It is probably most common in the calves, but can occur in any large muscles, for instance in the thighs, back, neck or abdomen. It can occur suddenly, often without warning and can be frightening for children the first time it occurs.

AROMATHERAPY

In order to improve the local circulation and so bring in more blood and oxygen to the muscles, massaging the area is often very beneficial. Firm effleurage, or stroking movements, are particular helpful, always done in a direction towards the heart. To aid this action, diluted essential oils like Juniper, Lavender, Marjoram, Rosemary or even Black Pepper should be used. These are all rubefacient, meaning they dilate the local blood vessels and encourage increased blood flow. The muscles become warmed and relaxed. For frequent leg cramps for instance, regular massage of the legs and thighs with one or more of these oils can help a good deal.

HERBALISM

One of the most effective treatments for cramp is the aptly named Cramp Bark (European

To ease stiff, aching arm muscles, oil the arm and then massage deeply down the length of the arm with the thumbs.

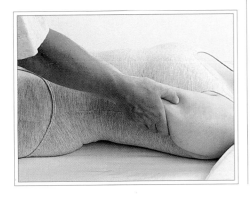

CAUSES OF CRAMP

A major factor is inadequate circulation to the muscles, especially if cramp comes on with exercise or effort (see also Poor Circulation, page 51); with athletes or people doing hard physical work there may also be a problem of salt deficiency from excessive sweating.

Repetitive movements, such as typing, can provoke cramping and lead on to inflammation – repetitive strain injury is a potential consequence of overuse of a set of muscles in this way. Night cramps are probably due to a combination of reduced circulation, tiredness and stress, and the whole person needs to be treated.

Cranberry Bush) *(Viburnum opulus)*, better known to gardeners as the guelder rose. The bark is made into a tincture (see page 14) that is almost a specific remedy for muscle spasms, both internally in instances of, say, period pains or abdominal cramps, and used locally for leg cramps. Either make a warm compress using the tincture diluted about 1:4 with hot water, or incorporate it into a cream (see page 16) and massage into the affected areas. Internally, take 5 ml (1 tsp) once or twice daily, ideally in a little hot water. It is very effective, but unpleasant! For reduced circulation leading to cramping sensations, you may also find it helpful

to drink Ginger *(Zingiber officinalis)* tea, especially in the evening for helping night cramps.

HOMEOPATHY

Some possible remedies are:

COLCHICUM: for cramps usually in the soles of the feet.

CUPRUM MET: for severe cramps, often starting in the toes or fingers and spreading up the limb; symptoms are aggravated by cold winds, and often come on in the evening.

GELSEMIUM: for writer's cramp, especially if associated with mental exhaustion or tension.

NUX VOMICA: this is most often used for digestive problems due to over-eating, but can be helpful for night cramps.

NATUROPATHY

When a cramp occurs, the first self-help action needs to be to stretch the affected muscle; for example if the calf muscle has gone into spasm, it can be relieved by pushing down with the heel to elongate the muscle again, even though this initially feels very painful! If taking hard physical exercise in very hot weather, there may be a case for ensuring you have more salt in the diet, although this should be temporary and not overdone.

Using alternate hot and cold compresses on the affected areas is another way to improve local circulation in cases of repeated cramps. For long-term problems look at one of the many relaxation techniques around.

FIBROSITIS

This is inflammation of the muscle fibres, often a chronic condition which can lead to the formation of hard nodules within the muscle. Fibrositis particularly affects the large muscles of the back, neck and shoulders, and sometimes into the buttocks. It may occur as a result of an injury, but is equally likely to arise from chronic stress and tension or poor posture. It needs to be differentiated from arthritis or other causes of pain.

AROMATHERAPY

Massage of the affected area is one of the most effective forms of treatment, and professional massage may well be needed to get deep into the tight muscles. At home, stroking and kneading the muscles with an oil containing essential oils of Eucalyptus, Lavender, Marjoram, Pine or Rosemary will help to warm and relax the affected fibres, stimulating the local circulation.

HERBALISM

Any anti-inflammatory herbs that might be taken internally can often be used in conjunction with local agents, for instance the oils suggested above. Furthermore, since stress is often a factor, look at herbs for easing tension generally (see Stress, pages 28-9). A couple of herbs that may be appropriate to take are Meadowsweet *(Filipendula ulmaria)* as an infusion, or Willow Bark *(Salix alba)* taken as a decoction (see page 12), unless tablets are available. Both these plants contain substances that are related chemically to aspirin; indeed this was first synthesized from extracts of Willow, and was named after an older Latin name for Meadowsweet, *Spiraea*. They are, however, much safer for the stomach, notably Meadowsweet, but seek advice before using if you are allergic to aspirin.

MEADOWSWEET
(Filipendula ulmaria)

HOMEOPATHY

In the first place try Rhus tox if the pains are aggravated when first starting to move after resting, but gradually ease with continued steady movement. For other suggestions see Rheumatism, pages 88-9.

NATUROPATHY

Massage, stretching exercises and attention to posture will all help greatly, as will proper rest and relaxation. See a Naturopathy therapist for the best advice which will suit your own health and lifestyle.

MASSAGE FOR FIBROSITIS

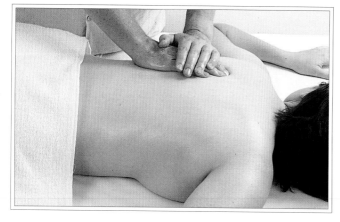

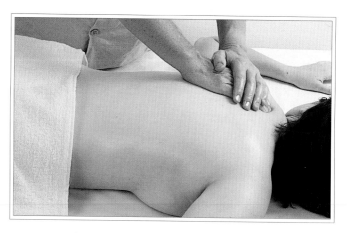

1 To ease stiff muscles in the shoulder, oil the back, using a base oil and essential oils as recommended. Place fingers just inside the shoulder blade, supporting with the other hand. Keep a relaxed but firm pressure.

2 Move fingers steadily around the shoulder blade, pressing in firmly but within comfort limits. Repeat several times. Ease the pressure if too uncomfortable. Try this massage daily for a week.

GOUT

This condition occurs when there is an excess of uric acid in the body, and the kidneys cannot get rid of it effectively. The acid crystallizes into tiny sharp deposits like miniature needles; these collect in joints, often in the toes or feet but sometimes elsewhere such as the earlobes, causing intense pain and inflammation. The first signs of an attack may in fact be a feverish feeling, before the joint swells.

AROMATHERAPY

In an acute attack it is definitely not appropriate to massage the affected area – there is too much inflammation. Instead, use oils in cool or cold compresses to reduce the discomfort. For a detoxifying effect, try Cypress, Fennel, Juniper, Lemon or Pine oils. These may also be used in the bath. As the swelling and inflammation reduce, perhaps switch to oils such as Lavender or Rosemary for inducing local warmth and flushing toxins out of the joints.

HERBALISM

The classic herb is undoubtedly Celery Seed (*Apium graveolens*); this may be taken in tablet form or by making a tea from 5 ml (1 tsp) of the seeds, lightly crushed with the back of a spoon, in 300 ml (½ pt/1¼ cups) of boiling water. Take 2 to 3 cupfuls a day for acute attacks of gout, to encourage strongly the excretion of uric acid. More directly anti-inflammatory herbs

CELERY SEED (*Apium graveolens*)

SELF-HELP FOR GOUT

Uric acid may accumulate within the kidneys themselves, leading to kidney stones, which may have to be surgically removed. Generally speaking, all the advice for Arthritis (see pages 83-4), will be applicable to gout.

An acute attack of gout is extremely painful and may require medical treatment. Try reducing food to a minimum but make sure to drink plenty of water, which will encourage removal of uric acid from the body.

---

such as Meadowsweet (*Filipendula ulmaria*), Willow Bark (*Salix alba*) or Devil's Claw (*Harpagophytum procumbens*) may be taken alongside the Celery Seed.

The first two are described under Fibrositis (see page 86) while Devil's Claw is widely available in tablets or capsules, which are probably the easiest method in which to take it, up to 3 g per day. A general cleansing herb which is excellent to use regularly for chronic gout is Nettle (*Urtica dioca*) – simply drink it as a tea, 1 or 2 cups a day for a month or so.

HOMEOPATHY

A couple of remedies that often give some relief are:
ARNICA: for repeated attacks of gout, especially affecting the big toe, with

DEVIL'S CLAW
(*Harpagophytum procumbens*)

hot, painful and very tender joints.
RHUS TOX: a versatile remedy for most rheumatic or arthritic problems; suitable for hard, painful swelling of the joints – these can be mistaken in mild attacks for a bunion.

NATUROPATHY

Use cold compresses (see page 15) to reduce the swelling, switching to hot/cold applications in the longer term to encourage better circulation around the joint. Increase vegetable intake, especially raw or juiced, for a more alkaline intake, and cut out cheese, red wine (in the short term all alcohol), red meats, coffee and strong tea. When the swelling and inflammation has subsided, increase exercise to maintain joint mobility.

Drink plenty of mineral or spring water to encourage kidney action. Pain can be eased with some of the herbs discussed above.

RHEUMATISM

This is a general term which covers any inflammatory process in the muscles or joints; here its meaning will be limited to muscular rheumatism as Arthritis has already been covered (see pages 83-4). Much of the advice for Fibrositis (see page 86) is also relevant here as this is sometimes simply placed under the heading of rheumatism.

AROMATHERAPY

To aid the cleansing of the tissues, essential oils are probably best used in the bath (see page 8); appropriate oils are Cypress, Juniper, Pine and Rosemary, while Lavender may be added for greater muscle relaxation. Lavender and Rosemary are in addition quite analgesic in effect, giving some welcome relief from the pains and stiffness. If not too uncomfortable, massaging in a choice from these two, or else Juniper or Marjoram, diluted to 2 per cent in a base vegetable oil, speeds up the removal of toxins and

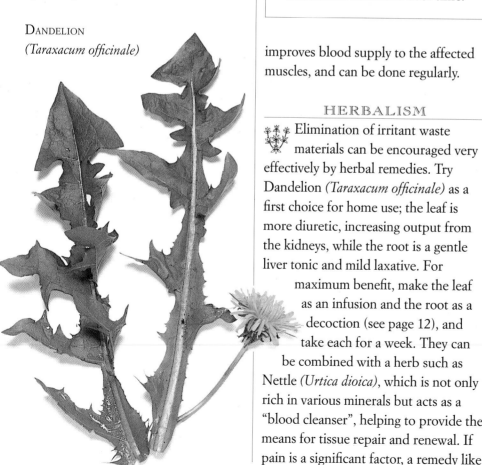

DANDELION
(*Taraxacum officinale*)

RHEUMATISM
As a rule, the emphasis of natural treatments is placed even more on detoxifying the system than is the case with joint problems, removing waste matter that congests and irritates the muscles to allow greater freedom of movement. A combination of dietary changes, exercise within limits of comfort, and other natural methods outlined in this section can dramatically improve rheumatic disorders over time.

improves blood supply to the affected muscles, and can be done regularly.

HERBALISM

Elimination of irritant waste materials can be encouraged very effectively by herbal remedies. Try Dandelion (*Taraxacum officinale*) as a first choice for home use; the leaf is more diuretic, increasing output from the kidneys, while the root is a gentle liver tonic and mild laxative. For maximum benefit, make the leaf as an infusion and the root as a decoction (see page 12), and take each for a week. They can be combined with a herb such as Nettle (*Urtica dioica*), which is not only rich in various minerals but acts as a "blood cleanser", helping to provide the means for tissue repair and renewal. If pain is a significant factor, a remedy like

GINGER (*Zingiber officinalis*)

Meadowsweet (*Filipendula ulmaria*) can be very useful. These last two herbs can be used as infusions for a couple of weeks; for persistent discomfort get professional treatment.

If the circulation is definitely restricted, and the aching and stiffness are made worse by damp, cold weather, add a small amount of fresh Ginger (*Zingiber officinalis*) to any infusion. Ginger root is a strong circulatory stimulant and has a large part to play in treating many rheumatic/arthritic disorders.

HOMEOPATHY

Here are a few potentially helpful remedies; also compare with the suggestions for other conditions in this section which may be appropriate.
ACTAEA RAC: particularly good for painful, stiff muscles in the back and neck; also good for aching muscles after exercise or for neuralgic pains.
ARNICA: for general aching of limbs, with a feeling of being bruised (see also First Aid section, page 102).

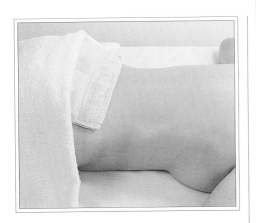

Compresses can stimulate circulation and reduce inflammation.

BRYONIA: for stiffness and swelling, for instance of the hands and arms; if the joints feel uncomfortable and "crack" with movement, this remedy may well be very useful too.

RHUS TOX: for the typical stiffness pattern of rheumatic disorders, aggravated after resting and improving after some movements. The remedy for lumbago, with low back pains on rising or after long periods of sitting.

RUTA GRAV: for pains felt in the tendons and muscles, and joints such as wrists, knees and ankles. May also be helpful in relieving sciatic pains (see page 25).

ARNICA (*Arnica montana*)

RUE (*Ruta graveolens*)

NATUROPATHY

Often a good soak in a hot bath (perhaps with a handful of Epsom salts) eases the stiffness and aching of muscular rheumatism, but too frequent a use of hot applications may produce too much congestion, so try alternating hot/cold compresses, if you can, in order to stimulate blood flow. A brisk rub with a thick, coarse towel will certainly aid this process. It is important to keep active as far as possible, so exercise is to be encouraged within individual limits of ability. Diet should be aimed at reducing acid waste matter, with plenty of vegetables and fresh fruit (with the probable exception of oranges) and very little refined carbohydrates or sugary foods. A supplement may be useful: take a multi-vitamin and mineral tablet once a day, or else initially just take a Vitamin B supplement. In winter, especially in cooler climates, taking a fish oil supplement such as cod liver oil capsules may ease stiffness.

THE SKIN

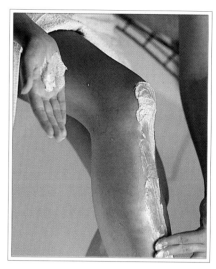

The natural approach to skin problems starts by taking the view that most disorders of the skin reflect inner imbalance, and that the whole person needs to be treated for truly effective results. This is especially so in conditions such as eczema or psoriasis, which can be highly complex disorders requiring professional treatment on an individual basis. Chronic or persistent problems should be referred to a practitioner. Given the potential negative effects of orthodox treatments such as steroid cream for eczema, there is much to be gained by looking at natural therapies.

The traditional treatment of many skin problems involves considerable attention being paid to the cleansing of the whole body. Both Western and Eastern (for example, Chinese or Indian) systems of herbal medicine have developed successful strategies for treating the skin. The role of other factors such as hormone balance, stress and lowered vitality also needs to be considered; for self-help other sections of this book may therefore be very useful.

As with all the conditions discussed in this book, do not overdo any of the self-help treatments suggested; if any skin problems get worse or continue for more than a short time, then stop the treatment and/or get professional help. Do not mix therapies; this is particularly true of homeopathy since the pattern of individual symptoms will be affected by other treatments, making the choice of homeopathic remedy more difficult. Small is beautiful in all the therapies – if a dose of something is helpful, do not think that doubling the dose will have double the benefit; quite often it is the opposite!

ABOVE: Herbal creams and ointments can bring relief to problem skin sufferers.

ABSCESS

An abscess is a localized inflamed swelling, containing pus. Abscesses can develop externally on the skin, but also internally in the mouth or on other mucous membranes – these should be referred for qualified medical treatment. Treatments locally on the skin will generally involve hot compresses or poultices to draw out the toxic waste matter; recurrent abscesses often indicate a weakened immune system. See also Boils, page 95.

AROMATHERAPY

Apply a hot compress (see page 15) to the area, by adding 5-6 drops of essential oil to a bowl of water as hot as you can bear, and soaking a piece of absorbent material in it. Suitable materials include lint, a clean handkerchief, or a face flannel. Fold over a couple of times for a thicker pad, and place on the abscess, covering with a bandage or piece of cling film (plastic-wrap) to hold in position. Renew when cooling to body temperature, and keep on for at least 30 minutes.

Appropriate essential oils for this process are Bergamot, Chamomile, Lavender and Tea Tree, either separately or in a combination such as Bergamot for its antiseptic properties, together with Lavender (also antiseptic) for a greater anti-inflammatory effect. (Remember that the number of drops suggested is the *total* amount used, not the number for each herb.)

HERBALISM

Make a hot poultice (see page 15) from a herb such as Marshmallow (*Althea officinalis*) for external treatment of the area. Either pour boiling water on to some fresh leaves, or mix the powdered root with hot water to make a paste. It may be helpful to use a little oil on the skin first to stop the poultice sticking, then place the herb on the abscess and cover with a clean gauze or strips of cotton, holding in position as above. Such a poultice can be kept on for several hours, but

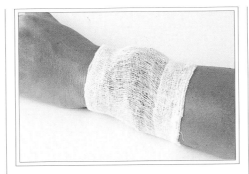

Apply a hot poultice on to the affected area, applying a little base oil to the skin first so that the poultice does not stick.

may need replacing every couple of hours. Another excellent herb to help draw out pus is Slippery Elm (*Ulmus fulva*); use the powdered inner bark as for the Marshmallow root above.

For mouth abscesses, it may be appropriate simply to place a hot compress, made with an infusion of Chamomile (*Chamomilla recutita*), on the cheek over the area until a doctor or dentist can be seen. Internal treatment, as described under Boils (see page 95), will be most helpful in cleansing the system as a whole and boosting immunity.

HOMEOPATHY

Hot compresses are likely to be suggested by practitioners here too, perhaps using tinctures of Hypericum or Calendula. Pour 15 ml (1 tbsp) of hot water on to 2 drops of either remedy, and soak a piece of

gauze in it. Place on the area and cover, renewing when cooling down.

Internally, take a few doses of either Hepar sulph if the abscess is hot, throbs with pain and is very tender to the touch, or else Silica if the abscess, although equally painful, feels cold to the touch, and the discharge is slow to clear up. These two remedies are very good for suppurating (oozing) skin conditions generally, given their different symptom pictures.

NATUROPATHY

If nothing else is available, use just hot water to make a compress, or put a hot water bottle over the affected area. You can use cabbage leaves from the garden with excellent results; take a few of the outer leaves, cut out the central rib and coarsely chop the leaves, pour on boiling water and make a poultice as outlined above. This is very soothing and helps to draw out infection. You may obtain Kaolin from a pharmacist to make a poultice, spread on a dressing and use over the area. When an abscess bursts, cover with a sterile dry dressing. For repeated problems a programme of dietary reform will be most helpful; for further information, see Boils, page 95.

MARSHMALLOW (*Althea officinalis*)

ACNE

This is a very common skin condition during puberty, although it may continue into later life for some people. Increasing levels of hormones during adolescence lead to greater activity of the skin's sebaceous glands, and if this becomes too great, excessive amounts of sebum, our natural oily skin lubricant, are produced. This in turn can cause the glands and hair follicles to become blocked and infected.

AROMATHERAPY

Many essential oils are not only antiseptic but also promote healing or generation of new healthy skin cells. Some of the best are Bergamot, Geranium, Lavender and Lemon; these may need to be used in varying combinations depending on the state of the skin and the person as a whole. Bergamot, for instance, is an effective antidepressant, and this emotional quality may be helpful at times as acne can understandably make the sufferer feel low (adolescence is a time of fluctuating self-esteem at the best of times), and as an astringent, antiseptic oil it is excellent for greasy, infected skin. Do not, however, overuse this oil as it increases the skin's sensitivity to the sun; moderate amounts of sunlight are generally good for drying and healing the skin too.

These oils may be used in a light carrier vegetable oil such as Grapeseed, which has a

WITCH HAZEL (*Hamamelis virginiana*)

SELF-HELP FOR ACNE

The most common reaction of most people is to squeeze the spots; this almost always serves to spread the infection into surrounding tissues, and if done repeatedly can damage the local skin areas, producing scarring. Any programme of treatment therefore needs to include a lot of self-help to be successful. The natural therapies offer the most successful and safest ways to improve the condition and rebalance of the skin.

The best approach is to combine local, external cleansing with internal treatment; all therapies are likely to emphasize the importance of diet in treating acne.

Where acne persists for years after adolescence, there may well be a hormonal imbalance that needs to be addressed, and again there are appropriate natural remedies that may be used – seek professional treatment if needed.

slight astringency of its own, or Coconut, or else mixed into gentle cleansing creams for regular use on the affected areas. Another base might be a toning lotion such as triple-distilled Rosewater, Orange Blossom water or perhaps distilled Witch Hazel for extra astringency. Use 1-2 per cent of essential oils in any of these base carriers. If there is much

evidence of scarring after the condition has improved, use the essential oils in a carrier which includes 10 per cent Wheatgerm oil to promote skin elasticity and healing.

HERBALISM

Initial treatment should be firmly geared towards cleansing of the skin and of the whole system. Locally, any of the essential oils described above may be used, or else cleanse the skin with an infusion of herbs (see page 12) such as Elderflower (*Sambucus nigra*), Lavender (*Lavandula vera*) or Marigold (*Calendula officinalis*); adding 5 ml (1 tsp) of distilled Witch Hazel (*Hamamelis virginiana*) to 300 ml (½ pt/1¼ cups) of the infusion will gently increase the astringency if needed.

The main use of herbal remedies though will be internally: choose a mixture of the following herbs: BURDOCK (*Arctium lappa*): a powerful tissue cleanser, encouraging the removal of waste matter from the skin via the blood supply, and equally helping the transport of nutrients to the skin. The root is more powerful, and a decoction should be used (see page 12), the leaf is made into an infusion.

Start by taking small amounts of this herb (about 45 ml (3 tbsp), 3 times a day) as it can initially stir things up and the skin seems to get worse.
CONE FLOWER (*Echinacea angustifolia* or *E. purpurea*): the best all-purpose immune stimulant, aiding resistance

MARIGOLD *(Calendula officinalis)*

and speeding up our reactions to infection. Used together with the above herbs, this creates a strong detoxification process.

DANDELION *(Taraxacum officinale)*: the root in particular is helpful in improving the detoxifying action of the liver, and also as a gentle laxative, taking pressure away from the skin as an organ of elimination.

RED CLOVER *(Trifolium pratense)*: another excellent blood and tissue cleanser, the infusion can also be used externally to carefully bathe inflamed spots and is gentle

---

ACNE AND THE ADOLESCENT
Acne can be a major blight on adolescence, causing much emotional upset and even relationship difficulties, so it is important that familes and all concerned do not exaggerate the condition. Concern and practical help are better then either dismissing the problem or worst still, making negative comments. Gentle, but regular, cleansing of the skin, attention to hygiene and diet will all help keep acne to a minimum, so encouragement of these activities is useful, even if met with opposition!

---

enough to use on children in this way. *REMEMBER*: if using more than one herb in an infusion or a decoction, the amount of each herb included is reduced to maintain the given overall maximum amounts.

HOMEOPATHY

In the short term try one of these remedies (also refer to the remedy suggestions for Abscesses and Boils, pages 91 and 95).

CALC SULPH: for spots that never come to a real head, but get tender and inflamed and then seem to subside after a while (suitable for "blind boils").
HEPAR SULPH: for lots of pus-filled spots, which feel hot and tender to the touch, and generally unhealthy-looking skin.
SILICA: for slow-healing of the skin, spots that develop pus which is slow to clear; this remedy is particularly good for helping the healing of scarring.

NATUROPATHY

The first basic principle of the naturopathic approach (as with all the other natural therapies) is to overhaul the diet, as far as is

---

possible given teenage fads! A reduction of sugary, fatty foods is essential, shifting the balance towards fresh fruit and vegetables, whole grains and lean forms of protein. It is often desirable to reduce dairy products for a while, especially milk or strong cheeses. Taking plenty of fluids regularly is important, *not* fizzy drinks or tea and coffee, but water or fruit juices. Alcohol should also be reduced.

Stimulating the circulation, either by self-massage or using hydrotherapy – for instance, by briskly rubbing the trunk and limbs with a loofah dipped in cool water – is a helpful aid to cleansing of the skin. Allow the skin to breathe by wearing cool clothes, and pay strict attention to hygiene. Sunshine is usually helpful, although be careful not to stay in the sun too long, and take adequate sun-protection measures.

Supplementation of the diet can speed up the cleansing/ healing processes initially; important vitamins are A (around 2,500 iu daily), B complex and C (up to 300 mg daily), while one of the most useful minerals is zinc (up to 15 mg daily). Evening Primrose oil has been found to be of benefit in some cases; take up to 1,500 mg daily.

RED CLOVER *(Trifolium pratense)*

ATHLETE'S FOOT

This fungal skin condition can be produced by a number of different microscopic fungal growths, causing inflammation and itching. Despite its name, it is neither confined to the feet nor only restricted to athletes!

AROMATHERAPY

The most suitable anti-fungal essential oils to use are Lavender, Myrrh and Tea Tree, all of which not only tackle the infection directly but are also soothing and healing. Initially they may be best applied dissolved in a little neat alcohol, at 2-3 per cent dilution, or even used sparingly on their own on the moist, infected skin; when the skin is drier, they might then be incorporated into a cream base, up to 3 per cent dilution (see page 16).

Another useful base is Olive oil, which in itself seems to have some anti-fungal activity (see also Thrush, pages 74-5). Oil of Calendula, or the Old English Marigold, has very helpful healing properties and may be used as a base too. It may be helpful in the beginning to use a footbath, with 10 drops of one of the essential oils mentioned, but it is essential that the feet are dried thoroughly afterwards, and kept aired as often as possible.

MARIGOLD *(Calendula officinalis)*

SELF-HELP MEASURES

The commonest sites are where the skin gets moist and hot, such as between the toes or in the groin, and on the scalp where it may take the form of ringworm.

The most important self-help measures involve keeping the affected area cool and dry, and paying scrupulous attention to hygiene as the fungus can accumulate under the nails causing infection between the fingers or simply spreading by contact.

HERBALISM

External applications of tinctures of either Marigold *(Calendula officinalis)* or Myrrh *(Commiphora molmol)* are powerfully anti-fungal; leave the application to dry out on the skin. If the skin is very moist, these two herbs may be applied in powder form if available, either neat or by mixing with unperfumed talcum powder.

Widespread or recurrent infection may also require internal remedies to bolster the immune system – take Garlic *(Allium sativum)* regularly, either in food or perhaps as a capsule; a short course of Cone Flower *(Echinacea angustifolia* or *E. purpurea)*, as an infusion, tincture (see pages 12 and 14 respectively) or in tablets (around 1,500 mg per day) may help.

CONE FLOWER *(Echinacea angustifolia)*

HOMEOPATHY

Homeopaths may well also recommend Calendula as a local treatment, the tincture at first and then perhaps the oil or an ointment. Internal remedies will depend on the nature of the condition – for instance, if the area is moist and suppurating, a choice may be made from Hepar sulph, Merc sol, Silica or Sulphur, among others, so it is most advisable to seek a qualified practitioner.

NATUROPATHY

The first action to take is to ensure that the affected area keeps as dry and well-ventilated as possible, as the fungi responsible love hot, damp conditions. Use cotton socks and underwear, changing the garments daily. Ideally avoid wearing trainers and use leather shoes. Wash feet and other affected areas at least once a day, drying very thoroughly by patting dry rather than rubbing and chafing the skin. Use talcum powder to help keep the feet dry. Wash underwear in very hot water; the fungi may survive a low temperature wash cycle. Do not share towels or flannels as the infection may be passed on through physical contact. Footbaths can have 10-20 ml (2-4 tsp) of cider vinegar added, for a stronger anti-fungal effect.

BOILS

A boil is an acute inflamed and infected area on the skin, often in a blocked hair follicle. If a number of boils occur together, they may produce a large inflamed lump with several pus-filled "heads", and are termed a carbuncle (the medical term for a boil is a furuncle; if they are recurring, you are suffering from furunculosis). A stye is effectively a boil occurring in the base of an eyelash.

SLIPPERY ELM (*Ulmus fulva*)

AROMATHERAPY

In order to keep the tissues surrounding the boil clean and free from bacterial infection, it is very useful to wash the area 2 to 4 times a day with a 2 per cent dilution of essential oil of Lavender in cooled, boiled water, using sterile cotton wool (cotton pad) if possible. For drawing out the boil, a hot compress (see page 15) with oils such as Bergamot, Chamomile, Lavender or Tea Tree will be useful. These are variously antiseptic, anti-inflammatory and speed up healing; they may additionally be used in the bath as more general detoxifying remedies. The oil of choice would probably be Lavender; this is the most versatile oil to have for home use.

CAUSES OF BOILS

Boils tend to occur when people are run-down, either by stress or through poor diet and hygiene, but can be more frequent in some other illnesses, such as diabetes when the higher blood sugar levels provide food for bacteria (see also treatment suggestions for Abscess and Acne, pages 91 and 92-3). Generally, treatments are geared initially towards bringing the boil to a head and allowing it to burst and discharge the pus. It is important that all external applications are as clean as possible – for example, use sterile dressings for applying any poultices. In the medium to longer term, the natural therapies are ideally suited to cleansing the system as a whole, building up immunity to further outbreaks and restoring health and vitality.

Deeper causes of lowered vitality, such as prolonged stress, will need attention too, and oils may be used in the bath or in massage to help restore normal functioning. For additional help with stress, see pages 28-9.

BURDOCK (*Arctium lappa*)

LAVENDER (*Lavandula angustifolia*)

HERBALISM

Treatment from a herbal practitioner will focus internally as well as on any local applications, and this is also a good approach for self-help – if boils recur or resist home treatments, seek professional advice. Many herbs are soothing and anti-inflammatory when used as a poultice (see page 15); two excellent ones are Slippery Elm (*Ulmus fulva*) and Marshmallow (*Althea officinalis*).

Slippery Elm has been called the "herbalists' knife" for its ability to bring a boil to bursting point; simply thicken the powder with a little boiling water and apply as a paste, as hot as you can bear. Powdered Marshmallow root can also be used, or else the fresh leaves can be softened with boiling water and applied as a hot poultice. When the boil has burst, wash the area with cooled Lavender (*Lavandula vera*) tea or else keep using Slippery Elm as a cool poultice to speed up healing. If no other herbs are available, use fresh Garlic (*Allium sativum*) on the inflamed area, gently rubbing a cut clove over the skin.

Internally, Garlic may also be helpful, as a powerful antibiotic and immune-booster. Blood-cleansing herbal remedies include Burdock (*Arctium lappa*), Yellow Dock (*Rumex crispus*) and/or Dandelion Root (*Taraxacum officinale*), all most effectively taken as decoctions (see page 12), and Cleavers (*Galium aparine*) or Red Clover (*Trifolium pratense*) made as infusions (see page 12). It may be valuable to take Cone Flower (*Echinacea angustifolia* or *E. purpurea*) tablets or drops for a couple of weeks afterwards to help restore natural immune function.

HOMEOPATHY

Remedies to choose from are:

BELLADONNA: for very reddened skin probably in the earlier stages of developing a boil when it is throbbing and feels burningly hot to the touch.

HEPAR SULPH: for a hot, pus-filled boil which is coming to a head; this remedy will help it to mature and burst.

SILICA: this remedy is appropriate when the boil, although painful, feels if anything cold to the touch. This remedy

MARSHMALLOW (*Althea officinalis*)

and the previous one, with their differing symptom patterns, can be thought of as the "homeopath's knife", helping the boil to discharge.

NATUROPATHY

The diet definitely needs to be overhauled in the short term at least, to clear waste matter out of the system and provide essential nutrients for the immune defences to do their job properly and to aid tissue healing. If possible, try to have a strict diet for a week, cutting out all sugar, refined carbohydrates, tea,

GARLIC (*Allium sativum*)

coffee, alcohol, cheese and fried foods; eat plenty of fresh vegetables, raw or cooked fresh fruit, whole grains and a little lean protein.

Fluids should mostly be water, especially spring water, or else fruit juices (diluted in hot weather) or herbal teas. Alcohol should be avoided if at all possible.

There may be a case for taking extra nutrients in the form of a supplement: if the diet has been poor for a while, take a high quality multi-vitamin and mineral supplement, or else try taking zinc, up to 25 mg daily for a week and then 15 mg daily for another month.

Locally, bathing the boil in hot water may bring it to a head, or use a hot poultice (see page 15) made from the outer leaves of a cabbage, roughly chopped.

If boils recur, or continue, then seek professional help.

Fresh green salad leaves can greatly assist in clearing out the system.

COLD SORES

These are caused by the virus herpes simplex, another strain of which produces genital herpes (although it may be the same virus behaving differently). This virus is able to lie dormant in our tissues almost indefinitely until conditions trigger off an attack; it is probable that nearly everybody has acquired this virus at an early age from another person, so the key factor is what allows the virus to multiply and erupt.

AROMATHERAPY

Some essential oils are excellent for local use, and at the earliest stage possible of an outbreak are probably the most effective treatment for cold sores. Particularly good are Bergamot, Eucalyptus, Lavender, Lemon and Tea Tree. These may be applied neat, using just 1 drop on a cotton bud (swab), but may be better if diluted in a little alcohol; for home use a spirit such as vodka will do very well: add 5 drops of essential oil to 5 ml (1 tsp) of alcohol and dab on frequently. Neat Lavender oil may be dabbed on a little later to speed up healing.

HERBALISM

Local applications of herbs are most effective when they are used in tincture form (see page 14), dabbed on to the cold sores frequently to dry and heal the area. Some of the best are Lavender (*Lavandula vera*), Marigold (*Calendula officinalis*), Myrrh (*Commiphora molmol*), Wild Indigo (*Baptisia tinctoria*) and Witch Hazel (*Hamamelis virginiana*).

Where the appearance of cold sores indicates overall exhaustion, the herb St John's Wort (*Hypericum perforatum*) is an excellent choice; the tincture can be used locally as above, and may be taken internally as a calming restorative for the nervous system, 20 drops 3 times a day. *CAUTION*: this herb increases sensitivity to sunlight, so avoid prolonged exposure to strong, bright sunshine while taking internally.

ATTACK TRIGGERS

One of the most common predisposing factors is the ordinary cold, hence the name, but any respiratory infection can trigger an attack, as can being generally run-down. Extremes of temperature, or exposure to strong sunshine are other possible causes.

When an attack does occur, small blisters come out on the lips or at the corner of the mouth. These form a crust and remain moist underneath for up to 10 days or so before drying out. They are highly infectious during all the moist, weeping stages.

HOMEOPATHY

For a first-time eruption, try one of the following remedies, for up to 5 days at 30c potency (see Introduction, page 10, for explanation of potencies). If cold sores persist or recur, see a homeopath.

NAT MUR: for cold sores associated with a swelling of the lip, possibly even causing a deep crack, the sores forming several blisters.

RHUS TOX: for when the corners of the mouth get sore and there is a burning sensation; the eruptions may also spread out on to the chin, and the remedy "picture" often includes a red tip to the tongue as part of the overall symptoms.

NATUROPATHY

A simple yet highly effective home remedy is to apply freshly squeezed lemon juice to the cold sore, at the first signs of the problem (since the zest contains the essential oil, there is an obvious connection with Aromatherapy treatment). For a drying effect, you may find good quality eau-de-Cologne dabbed on and left to dry can be useful. It is often helpful to take a short course of a Vitamin B complex supplement, backed up by zinc (10-15 mg daily), and Vitamin C (500 mg daily). This is especially true when cold sores are recurring frequently, since these nutrients help to boost the immune system generally, as well as enhancing our ability to cope with chronic stress.

ST JOHN'S WORT
(*Hypericum perforatum*)

ECZEMA

This is a complex skin condition, and in most instances will need professional treatment. The natural therapies have an extremely good record in treating people with eczema, and given the problems associated with the long-term, regular use of steroid creams, there is a lot to be said for looking at other options.

AROMATHERAPY

The most important thing to remember when trying to help ease eczema is to be as flexible as possible. You may well need to vary the oils, and change the way you use them, since the nature of the condition can be due to so many factors, and the skin can get better for a while with one oil and then may need something different as the symptoms change.

Some of the most useful oils to use on the skin are Chamomile, Geranium, Lavender, Lemon Balm (often listed as Melissa, the first part of its Latin name) and perhaps Rose. They should be used in at most a 1 per cent dilution initially, and can be incorporated in a light aqueous cream, or perhaps use a thicker cream, ointment or pure vegetable oil base if the skin is extremely dry or weakened (see page 16 for how to make creams and ointments). Try these oils one at a time at first, to see whether the skin reacts to any of them.

CHAMOMILE
(*Chamomilla recutita*)

LEMON BALM
(*Melissa officinalis*)

Another method for a larger area of eczema is to use the oils in a cool compress: start with just 5 drops to 500 ml (16 fl oz/2 cups) water.

HERBALISM

This is an area where herbal medicine can be highly effective, and nearly always involves internal treatment as well as any local applications. Apart from some of the oils mentioned above, creams or ointments made with Comfrey (*Symphytum officinale*) or Marigold (*Calendula officinalis*) can help to reduce inflammation and speed up healing. For the intense itching that often accompanies eczema one of the best herbs is Chickweed (*Stellaria media*); use the fresh herb to make a cream or ointment, or simply make an infusion and when cooled apply as a compress.

If the skin is weeping, then infusions of Heartsease (*Viola tricolor*), Red Clover (*Trifolium pratense*) or even Nettle (*Urtica dioica*) used in a similar way will help to dry the area. Applying Evening Primrose (*Oenothera biennis*) oil, either neat or in a cream base, can

CAUSES OF ECZEMA

Essentially, eczema is an allergic inflammation and irritation of the skin. There may be a fairly straightforward external cause – for instance, a reaction to nickel which is often found in cheaper jewellery, watch straps, zips (zippers), clips and so on. Cosmetics, perfumes and hair colourings are another source of potential allergens, and fur, feathers, mould spores or dust make up another major group of irritants. Occasionally people react badly to various plants, especially in bright sunlight, and keen gardeners need to be aware of possible dangers if they have sensitive skin.

For many eczema sufferers, however, any external irritants are secondary to inner factors. In what is termed atopic eczema, there is often a family history of eczema, asthma or hay fever (all similarly over-reactive disorders), and problem areas such as emotional upsets, stress and food intolerance play a bigger part in the individual's eczema pattern. Unravelling the particular combination of factors for each person is often a detective story, which is where seeking treatment from a qualified natural therapist can be so valuable, with their focus on the whole person.

EVENING PRIMROSE
(*Oenothera biennis*)

be very soothing and healing.

The traditional herbal approach to eczema focuses on cleansing the tissues, and this can yield very good results. Herbs with blood-cleansing or "alternative" properties include Red Clover and Nettle, as infusions, and Burdock (*Arctium lappa*) or Yellow Dock (*Rumex crispus*) as decoctions (see page 12). Two other herbs that are of value in removing toxins are Cleavers (*Galium aparine*) for improving elimination via the kidneys, and Dandelion Root (*Taraxacum officinale*) to tone the liver and gently open the bowels. The former should be used as an infusion and the latter as a decoction. Mixtures may be made from the above herbs. Do not use for more than 3 weeks and if the skin gets worse, reduce the dosage by half.

HOMEOPATHY

Since eczema can initially flare up with treatment, take just one dose of a 30c potency (see page 10) per week, selecting from the following remedies (if there is no improvement within a month, consult a qualified practitioner):

GRAPHITES: for a moist, weeping skin which forms scabs that easily break off. The discharge is sticky, and the exposed surface of the skin may also bleed. This condition may be anywhere, but typical areas are behind the ears or on the face.

RHUS TOX: for a dry, very intensely itching eczema, such as might occur on the hands and wrists. Often little blisters form in the patches of redness.

SULPHUR: for hot, dry and burningly irritating skin. There is acute itching, but scratching makes it very sore. Heat of any kind (for instance, hot baths or lying in bed) makes the irritation much worse.

NATUROPATHY

Given the importance of stress in aggravating many kinds of eczema, looking at relaxation techniques may be valuable (see also Stress, pages 28-9). With regard to diet, many foods can be potential problems, most notably dairy foods. Where eczema has been around from infancy, it is often very beneficial to try eliminating cow's milk, cheese and other dairy products from the diet for up to three weeks. Reducing sugar, spicy foods, coffee, tea and alcohol, and keeping food additives to a minimum are other potentially useful approaches. Taking a supplement of Vitamin B complex

HEARTSEASE (*Viola tricolor*)

DIETARY ADVICE
Specific dietary advice will obviously require professional consultation, as there may be particular foods which provoke or aggravate an individual's eczema. If the suggestions in the Naturopathy section do not radically improve the skin with 6-8 weeks, get professional advice.

can help, and sometimes Vitamin A (up to 5,000 iu for a month) is needed. Evening Primrose oil can be taken internally as well as used locally; to boost the essential fatty acids within the body, take up to 1,500 mg daily.

PSORIASIS

This is a skin disease where the skin cells start to grow too rapidly; the immature cells over-produce but fail to mature into proper keratin. The new cells grow more rapidly than the old dead layers can be shed and so thick, reddened patches form which are covered with a silvery scale. They can appear in patches almost anywhere, often on the outer surfaces of the elbows or knees, and in severe cases can cover the whole body.

AROMATHERAPY

Essential oils which help to reduce inflammation may help locally (see Eczema, pages 98-9), but it may be just as helpful to concentrate on lowering the stress levels. Thus oils may be added to the bath: choose from Bergamot, Chamomile, Geranium, Jasmine, Lavender, Neroli or Rose for their relaxing and/or uplifting qualities. Change the oils around depending on the emotional state, and be prepared for limited success and slow improvements in the skin! Do not despair, psoriasis is notoriously difficult to treat, and sufferers carry the possibility of a recurrence even after the skin has cleared.

HERBALISM

Traditionally, psoriasis was linked to liver sluggishness as well as stress, and so herbal liver tonics and tissue cleansers form an initial part of treatment. Look at the herbs discussed under Eczema, particularly Yellow Dock (*Rumex crispus*) and Dandelion Root (*Taraxacum officinale*). These may be combined and made as a decoction (see page 12), to stimulate bile flow and clear toxins out of the whole system. Nettle (*Urtica dioica*) is also valuable as a cleanser; ideally take the juice (available in some countries) or else combine in an infusion (see page 12), with Cleavers (*Galium aparine*) for added effect. Topically, the thickened skin can be encouraged to slough off by rubbing with moistened fine oatmeal. Marigold (*Calendula officinalis*) can be used in a

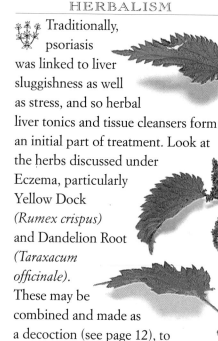

NETTLE (*Urtica dioica*)

SELF-HELP TREATMENT

Psoriasis can run in families, and is a very complex condition with no simple treatment. It is frequently aggravated by stress and by being run-down, and seems to be an example of an auto-immune disorder, that is, when the body's immune system fails to recognize its own cells and starts to react against itself. In nearly every case exposure to sunlight is helpful, and often the condition will disappear on a summer holiday, when sun and relaxation are combined.

RED CLOVER (*Trifolium pratense*)

cream or ointment to reduce the inflammation, or else Red Clover (*Trifolium pratense*) may be tried in similar fashion. If stress is an obvious factor, taking teas of gentle relaxants such as Chamomile (*Chamomilla recutita*), Lavender (*Lavandula vera*), Lemon Balm (*Melissa officinalis*) or Lime Blossom (*Tilia europaea*) over a period of time may help to restore balance.

HOMEOPATHY

Some short-term suggestions are:
ARSEN ALB: for roughened, scaly skin that may have a burning sensation, although often cold to the touch. The skin is exceptionally dry.
GRAPHITES: for when the skin dries out and cracks, producing a thick, sticky discharge. The cracked areas may also bleed, and the skin itches considerably.
SULPHUR: for hot, dry and itchy skin which is made worse by heat (although not necessarily the sun). Scratching gives very temporary relief, but then causes soreness and burning.

NATUROPATHY

Much of the dietary advice echoes that given under Eczema (see pages 98-9); there may be a case for looking at wheat as a source of food intolerance too; try eliminating suspected foods on a rotation basis, a couple of weeks or so off each food group. For a short while Vitamin A may be taken in quite high doses (up to 7,500 iu daily for 2-3 weeks), but this is stored in the liver and can be toxic in over-large amounts. A multi-vitamin supplement may give a gentler but safer effect over a long period of time.

Sunshine is most likely to benefit, but do not get sunburnt! It is still necessary to take sun-protection measures when exposing skin to sunlight for any prolonged period of time (see pages 110-11). The Dead Sea is famous as a treatment area for psoriasis, using the mineral salts from

Natural creams and oils can be gently massaged into affected areas of skin.

CLEAVERS *(Galium aparine)*

the sea together with sunbathing. These salts are now available in many countries, and can be added to the bath or a wash-basin to bathe smaller areas of skin. Evening Primrose oil may be of help, both locally and internally (take up to 1,500 mg daily). Relaxation techniques or classes can be important parts of self-help, learning how to cope with stress and not internalize it.

Due to the complexity of factors involved, psoriasis is not easily treated with self-help, and professional treatment may be the best course of action. It can be associated with other disorders, such as digestive problems, and may lead on to a specific form of arthritis, so read the suggestions under these headings (see pages 61 and 83-4) to see how the natural therapies can work on the whole person, and to suit your own condition.

Lime Blossom (Tilia europaea) *tea can help reduce stress levels.*

IMPROVING THE CONDITION

One cannot really say that psoriasis can be cured, but natural treatments can greatly improve the condition for long periods of time.

As psoriasis sufferers often have a tendency towards tense, insular personalities, the following Bach Flower Remedies (see page 102) can sometimes help: Agrimony, Crab Apple, Water Violet or Willow.

Whatever treatment is used, patience is required as visible improvement can take a while to show through.

FIRST AID

⟨❦⟩

There are a number of instances when natural remedies can be used for first-aid treatment, and you may find it useful to build up a natural first-aid kit, to go alongside items such as plasters, bandages and so on. The important feature to remember is that situations needing first-aid treatment are acute, so prompt help is essential, and also they should be limited in duration anyway, such as a bruise.

If symptoms get worse or persist, despite first aid, seek medical help. In this section some of the common problems that might arise are listed and possible forms of treatment identified.

A choice of items for a natural first-aid kit is up to each individual, but some excellent remedies are Comfrey ointment for bruises, sprains and strains; Lavender essential oil for burns, bruises, sprains and strains; Calendula cream (herbal or homeopathic) for cuts and grazes; homeopathic Arnica tablets at 6c or 30c potency for bruises and shock; and Rescue Remedy for all types of shock. The last is not technically part of mainstream herbalism, but is one of Dr Edward Bach's Flower Remedies. These are a series of gentle plant remedies which are intended to treat various emotional states, regardless of the physical disorder. For practical purposes, the Rescue Remedy is the finest treatment available for alleviating symptoms of shock.

Above: The distinctive smell of peppermint is highly effective when used as a smelling salt.

BITES AND STINGS

Bites and stings can occur from any number of insects, some being much more painful than others. In any situation where a bite or sting affects the mouth or even the throat, and also if there are signs of an allergic reaction, with distress and/or difficulty in breathing, get medical help immediately.

AROMATHERAPY

A drop of Lavender or Tea Tree oils may be applied to the area, ideally in a little iced water. This may be repeated every 10 minutes or so until the pain and irritation has subsided, or it can be made into a cold compress (see page 15) and left on for a couple of hours.

HERBALISM

A cold dressing made from an infusion (see page 12) of Chamomile (*Chamomilla recutita*), Elderflower (*Sambucus nigra*), Lavender (*Lavandula vera*) or Red Clover (*Trifolium pratense*) can be used over the area. Other herbal help can be to use fresh leaves of plants such as Lemon Balm (*Melissa officinalis*) or Plantain (*Plantago major* or *P. lanceolata*), or Yellow Dock (*Rumex crispus*) leaves – famous for treating nettle stings – directly on to the skin. Fresh onion may give quick relief from insect stings, placed over the

Use either water or a herbal infusion, with ice added. Wring out a cloth and hold over the inflamed area.

area. For continued irritation, apply a cream (see page 16) made with Chickweed (*Stellaria media*) or perhaps Marigold (*Calendula officinalis*). For bites, Marigold, Myrrh (*Commiphora molmol*) or St John's Wort (*Hypericum perforatum*) tinctures (see page 14) can help – use a drop or two neat on the bite or dilute 5 ml (1 tsp) into 15 ml (1 tbsp) of water for a cold dressing.

REMOVING A STING

Some stings, for instance from bees, result in the sting being left behind in the skin, and this should be carefully removed first. This is probably best done by flicking the sting out with a sharp knife; tweezers may be used, but these can result in squeezing the poison sac of the sting and thereby sending more toxin into the puncture hole.

HOMEOPATHY

Two classic remedies are Ledum, the remedy of choice for puncture wounds generally, or else Apis mel when there is much redness and swelling around the sting. Use 30c potency (see page 10), and take a dose every 20 minutes until the symptoms are much relieved. If there is a rash around the sting, apply a cold dressing using 2 drops of Urtica urens tincture to 15 ml (1 tbsp) of water. If there are symptoms of shock, the remedy to choose is Arnica, 1 dose per hour for 4 hours if needed.

CHICKWEED (*Stellaria media*)

NATUROPATHY

If possible, apply ice to the area as soon as possible to reduce inflammation and swelling. If the sting is from a bee, there may be some value in using diluted bicarbonate of soda to clean the area; conversely, if it is a wasp sting, it may be helpful to use diluted lemon juice or vinegar for the same purpose. Bites should be thoroughly cleaned before any treatment.

BRUISES

Bruises can happen for several reasons; a knock, crushed finger or toe, sprain or other injury are the normal causes. However, if bruising is severe, frequent and without obvious cause, then it may indicate a lack of Vitamin K, or even be a sign of diabetes or kidney disease; get professional advice if dietary changes (see below) do not help.

AROMATHERAPY

Immediate use of oil of Lavender, in an ice-cold compress, can be the most effective treatment to avoid swelling and widespread bruising. If a bruise has developed, at a later stage when it is changing colour and resolving, use Rosemary essential oil diluted in a vegetable oil base to massage gently into the tissues to increase local circulation and speed up the healing process.

HERBALISM

Ice-cold compresses can be made with distilled Witch Hazel (*Hamamelis virginiana*); either dilute 15 ml (1 tbsp) in 300 ml (½ pt/1¼ cups) of cold water and apply on a dressing, or else be prepared beforehand and keep some ice-cubes made with the Witch Hazel in a separately

WITCH HAZEL
(*Hamamelis virginiana*)

COMFREY *(Symphytum officinale)*

labelled bag in the freezer (this is a useful policy if you have children!). An infusion of Comfrey *(Symphytum officinale),* chilled with ice-cubes, can also be used for a cold compress. For aftercare, Comfrey oil or ointment (see page 16) is ideal, quickly healing the damaged tissues.

HOMEOPATHY

Probably the remedy of choice will be Arnica; this is excellent for any physical (or emotional) trauma and shock, and will help with bruising from a blow or injury. Take every 2 hours for up to 6 doses, then 3 times a day for 3 days, if needed. Keep an eye on symptoms; as they improve, reduce the frequency of dosage or stop taking the remedy altogether if much better. When the skin is unbroken, Arnica ointment may be applied to the bruised area; if there is damage to the skin, then Hypericum or Calendula ointments should be used instead. All the above ointments are available in most health shops. Other remedies for internal use could be Ruta grav or Rhus tox when the muscles, tendons or bones have been injured, for example in a sprain.

NATUROPATHY

Ice-cold compresses (see page 15) or packs should be applied as soon as possible – a bag of frozen peas makes a good temporary pack. If the bruise is severe or widespread, then try to raise the affected area to reduce local blood supply, and hence swelling. Repeated or very easy bruising may indicate Vitamin K deficiency; eat plenty of green vegetables such as broccoli, cabbage, spinach and so on, and also try taking plenty of live yoghurt to stimulate the gut flora that make this vitamin. To encourage dispersal of bruises, eat fresh pineapple, or drink the juice; it contains enzymes which aid this process. If bruises linger, it may be additionally helpful to take Vitamin C (500 mg daily for a few days).

ARNICA
(*Arnica montana*)

BURNS

Severe burns require urgent medical assistance; do not delay in getting treatment, especially for children and babies. The immediate treatment should be to apply cold water for up to 10 minutes if necessary, to reduce the heat. If the burn is from a chemical, remove any clothing that might have been affected. However, if there is burnt clothing stuck in the burn, then generally do not remove as this might do more damage.

AROMATHERAPY

Essential oil of Lavender is almost a specific treatment for burns; it is anti-inflammatory and analgesic, and promotes healing of the tissues. If applied quickly it can prevent scarring in many instances (I speak from personal experience). For a larger area put on to sterile gauze or smooth lint; otherwise drop on neat.

HERBALISM

In herbal practice Lavender (*Lavandula vera*) oil will most likely be used, as described above; another option for minor burns is Tea Tree (*Melaleuca alternifolia*) oil, a couple of drops applied to prevent blistering. If available, fresh Aloe vera gel is an excellent first-aid treatment for burns and scalds. Break open a leaf and spread the thick gel directly on to the

LAVENDER (*Lavandula vera*)

burn – again, this can produce completely scar-free healing if done as soon as possible. Other possibilities are infusions of Chamomile (*Chamomilla recutita*) or Marigold (*Calendula officinalis*), applied on a smooth dressing. Marigold cream (see page 16) may be used after some time has elapsed to ease continuing inflammation and soreness.

HOMEOPATHY

Probably the most-used homeopathic remedy for the first-aid treatment of burns is Arnica, followed by Cantharis; this helps to remove the burning pains that accompany blistering of the skin. For very minor burns Urtica urens may be suitable; probably only a couple of doses will be needed in this case. Urtica is also available as an ointment and is very effective for soothing superficial burns. Alternatively, after cooling of the skin it may be appropriate to use a commercial cream on a small burn.

CAUTION
Burns larger than the palm of your hand should be seen by a doctor immediately, regardless of any self-help treatment that has been advised here. All burns are painful and should be touched as little as possible.

MARIGOLD (*Calendula officinalis*)

REMEMBER, do not use greasy ointments, butter or other fats on new burns as all this does is simply fry the skin. Always cool the area thoroughly as the first treatment.

NATUROPATHY

Once the skin has been cooled, a valuable home remedy is honey; this is both antiseptic and promotes healing. When healing has started, a Vitamin E cream can aid restoration of tissue elasticity and reduce scarring. Do not give hot drinks to someone who has a burn; frequent small sips of cool water can help to replace lost fluids in more serious cases.

CHAMOMILE (*Chamomilla recutita*)

CUTS AND GRAZES

The first priority is to clean the area gently but thoroughly to remove any dirt. If the wound is deep, needing stitches, cover with a dry dressing and get medical help. It may be a sensible precaution to consider a tetanus jab (shot) if the cut has been from a dirty object or an animal, especially if there is a puncture wound.

AROMATHERAPY

The two oils of choice are probably Lavender and Tea Tree. These may be used neat on small cuts and scratches; they will sting temporarily but this soon passes. They can be added to a bowl of water for bathing (see page 8) and cleaning the affected area initially, or a couple of drops may be placed on a plaster or other clean dressing and applied over the site of the injury. Both these oils fight any infection as well as stimulating healing, and are generally very safe to use neat in this way.

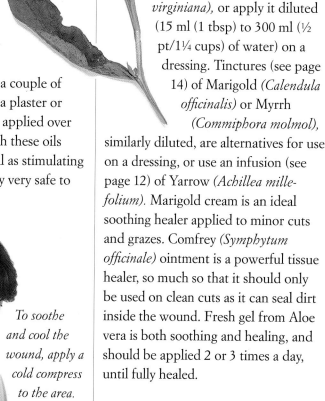

To soothe and cool the wound, apply a cold compress to the area.

COMFREY *(Symphytum officinale)*

HERBALISM

Wash the area with distilled Witch Hazel *(Hamamelis virginiana),* or apply it diluted (15 ml (1 tbsp) to 300 ml (½ pt/1¼ cups) of water) on a dressing. Tinctures (see page 14) of Marigold *(Calendula officinalis)* or Myrrh *(Commiphora molmol),* similarly diluted, are alternatives for use on a dressing, or use an infusion (see page 12) of Yarrow *(Achillea mille-folium).* Marigold cream is an ideal soothing healer applied to minor cuts and grazes. Comfrey *(Symphytum officinale)* ointment is a powerful tissue healer, so much so that it should only be used on clean cuts as it can seal dirt inside the wound. Fresh gel from Aloe vera is both soothing and healing, and should be applied 2 or 3 times a day, until fully healed.

HOMEOPATHY

Externally, a compress with either Hypericum or Calendula tinctures, 2 drops in 15 ml (1 tbsp) of water, may be used. This can be followed up by an

Add 2-3 drops of Lavender oil to a cold compress as a powerful antiseptic.

ointment from either of these (or any commercial cream made from both). Internally, take up to 4 doses of either Hypericum, especially if the injury has affected the fingers or toes and damaged local nerves, or Arnica for the shock of the injury, at 4-hourly intervals. For anything more serious get professional treatment.

NATUROPATHY

Clean your own hands thoroughly before cleaning the cut or graze, and apply a little honey or a Vitamin E cream on minor injuries. Keep the area covered if possible to avoid infection, and watch out for any swelling or inflammation.

YARROW *(Achillea millefolium)*

FAINTING

Feeling faint, or actually blacking-out, is due to a temporary lack of blood to the brain, and an isolated incident can be due to a number of immediate causes, such as excess heat or cold, fear, emotional upset, sight of blood, needles or something else that the person considers unpleasant.

AROMATHERAPY

For someone feeling faint, use one of the following oils like smelling salts, holding the bottle under the nose or else putting a couple of drops on a tissue and getting the person to breathe the aroma. Peppermint is particularly good, also Lavender, Neroli, Petitgrain and Rosemary. A drop gently massaged into the temples can be useful – a good commercial product for this use is Tiger Balm, which contains menthol and eucalyptol.

HERBALISM

Generally, any strong-smelling substance tends to stimulate the brain and relieve feelings of faintness. If available, tinctures (see page 14) of Lavender (*Lavandula vera*) or Peppermint (*Mentha piperita*) are pleasant and effective when used as smelling salts. One of the best remedies, especially when shock or upset has caused the faint feeling, is Rescue Remedy. If the person is conscious, put 4 drops under the tongue; if not, then moisten the lips with a couple of drops, and give 4 drops under the tongue when he or she comes round; repeat in half an hour if still feeling woozy.

HOMEOPATHY

Apart from the usual first-aid approach of making the person comfortable, if there is an obvious cause for the fainting, then a single dose of one of the following remedies may be called for.

ACONITE: for the effects of fright.
ARNICA: for faintness due to an accident, injury or shock.
IGNATIA: for over-excitement, or even feelings of hysteria.

POSTURAL HYPERTENSION

One of the commonest causes of fainting is postural hypotension (that is, a sudden change in position, such as standing up quickly), which lowers the blood pressure to the brain. Repeated fainting attacks call for expert investigation into the causes, which may range from low blood pressure or anaemia to changes in blood sugar levels. When someone has fainted, do not try to lift them up; falling down brings the head level with the heart and helps to bring blood to the brain more easily.

NUX VOMICA: for faint feelings associated with seeing blood, or from strong smells, or after a rich meal.
PULSATILLA: for the effects of being in a hot, stuffy atmosphere.

Finally, if the person has fainted, and on coming round feels chilly but desires fresh air, try a dose of Carbo veg – sometimes called the corpse reviver!

NATUROPATHY

Use basic first aid, such as ensuring there is enough fresh air if possible, helping the blood flow by sitting the person down and placing their head down between the knees, or else assisting them to lie down with their legs slightly raised. When recovering, give a few sips of water or better still warm peppermint tea.

FEELING FAINT

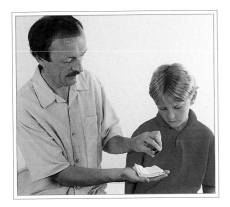

1 Put a couple of drops of essential oil on to a tissue.

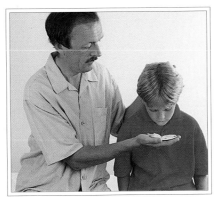

2 Hold the tissue under the nose and lean the head slightly forward.

N O S E B L E E D

This is most often due to a blow on the nose, rupturing some of the tiny blood vessels, and can be quite common in children. Occasionally a nosebleed is sparked off by very hot, humid weather, or by excitement, and if they occur frequently, professional treatment should be sought.

AROMATHERAPY

Soak a pad of cotton wool in cold, or even iced water with a couple of drops of Lemon oil added, and place firmly across the bridge of the nose. A more effective method is to place a small piece of this as a plug in the affected

Make an infusion of Yarrow (Achillea millefolium) *(see page 12). When cool, soak a piece of cotton wool or soft cloth in the infusion and place on the soft part of the nose. Hold firmly in place.*

nostril. The essential oil helps to speed up clotting. Sometimes placing a cold compress on the back of the neck can be helpful in reducing the local blood flow too.

HERBALISM

The herb of choice is Yarrow *(Achillea millefolium);* even its Latin name is derived from its supposed use by Achilles in stemming bleeding from his heel. Make an infusion (see page 12) and cool with ice-cubes, soak a pad in it and use as described under Aromatherapy above. The tincture (see page 14) can also be used, 15 ml (1 tbsp) in 300 ml (½ pt/1¼ cups) of cold water, as can distilled Witch Hazel *(Hamamelis virginiana).*
Traditionally, a leaf would be placed in the nostril to act as a plug, the finely divided leaflets

acting as a mesh for the blood platelets to produce a clot; however, removing this leaf often starts the nosebleed off again, so it is not particularly recommended.

HOMEOPATHY

Some useful remedies are:
FERRUM PHOS: for the results of a minor injury, or else from a head cold; a good remedy for childhood knocks.
HAMAMELIS: for profuse bleeding, with a feeling of pressure in the nose and sinus areas which is relieved by the blood loss to some extent.
PHOSPHORUS: for a heavy nosebleed associated with blowing the nose violently or sneezing, especially if occurring in the evening.

NATUROPATHY

In the first instance, get the person to sit down and lean forward slightly, pinching the soft part of the nose firmly between forefinger and thumb for several minutes. An ice-cube, or better still a pad of cotton wool soaked in iced water, can be held in place over this area too, to astringe the swollen blood vessels further.

CAUTION
In rare instances, conditions such as high blood pressure may be the reason behind the nosebleeds. Any unexplained or very heavy bleeds need immediate medical attention.

SPRAINS AND STRAINS

Asprain is an injury affecting a joint, with the tendons that attach muscles to the bones being overstretched and often torn. A strain is an injury to the muscles themselves, usually due to excessive or inappropriate exercise, lifting heavy weights and so on. The first treatment is a cold application (see Naturopathy entry below); massage of the area is not helpful at this stage, but can be used if the after-effects linger on.

AROMATHERAPY

The most useful essential oil is Lavender; use 5 drops to 15 ml (1 tbsp) of iced water for a compress. Chamomile oil may be used in the same way; where there is a sprain, try to keep the affected joint as still as possible initially to reduce internal bleeding and to allow healing to start as quickly as possible, ideally with the limb raised.

HERBALISM

Make an infusion of Comfrey leaves (*Symphytum officinale*) and apply as a cold compress (see page 15), or use diluted tinctures (see page 14) of Comfrey or Marigold (*Calendula*

When treating a strain, the colder the water for the compress, the more effective it will be for the strain.

officinalis), 15 ml (1 tbsp) to 300 ml (½ pt/1¼ cups) of cold water. When the swelling has subsided, gently rub in Comfrey ointment to speed up healing of the damaged fibres. If muscles ache through over-exercise, this ointment is a good home treatment with massage of the surrounding area twice a day.

HOMEOPATHY

Choose from these remedies:
ARNICA: for the results of a fall or accident, with soreness and also a feeling of shock.
RHUS TOX: for muscular strains, from lifting heavy weights for instance, with pain, stiffness and swelling.
RUTA GRAV: for torn ligaments or tendons, especially in sprains of the ankles or wrists, with a feeling of bruising in the bones.

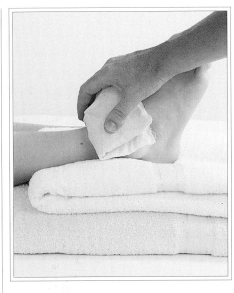

Raise the leg and support the ankle on something soft. Place an ice pack (a bag of frozen peas is a quick substitute) over the area and hold firmly in place.

NATUROPATHY

The immediate treatment is to apply the ICE approach : ice, compression and elevation. For example, a pack of frozen peas, held firmly around a sprained ankle, with the leg raised and supported, will help a good deal in reducing internal bleeding and joint swelling.

After the symptoms have subsided, there may be a case for using alternate hot and cold compresses (3 minutes hot followed by 1 minute cold, repeated for about 15 minutes) to improve local circulation to the relevant muscles, and later treatment may include massage to relieve muscular aches. Diluted oil of Lavender (about 2 per cent in a base oil) is helpful here.

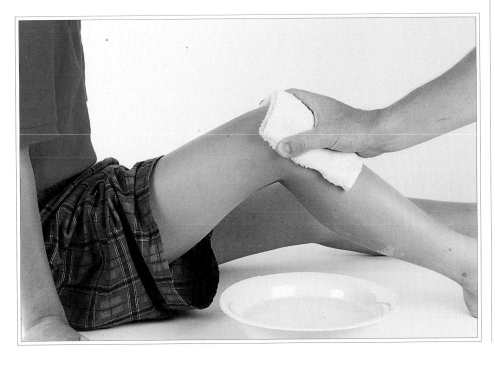

SUNBURN

In most respects sunburn should be treated as for Burns (see page 105). The first thing to do is to avoid further exposure to the sun until symptoms have been cleared. Severe sunburn can produce bad blistering, dehydration and sunstroke, and occasionally people have an allergic reaction to the sun's ultraviolet rays.

AROMATHERAPY

For mild, widespread sunburn use Chamomile oil, either in a bath, or add 5 drops to a small bowl of water and carefully dab on to unbroken skin. With children, essential oils for the bath should ideally be pre-diluted in 5 ml (1 tsp) of Sweet Almond or similar oil. If the sunburn is more severe, use Lavender oil in similar ways, or apply neat on to any blistered areas.

As aftercare for the dry, leathery-looking skin, use essential oils of Chamomile, Lavender, Rose or Sandalwood diluted at 2 per cent in a base oil such as Sweet Almond and gently massaged in twice daily. Very dry skin may benefit from the use of

ELDERFLOWER *(Sambucus nigra)*

THE RISK OF SKIN CANCER
An increasingly frequent sequel to excessive exposure to the sun is skin cancer, and reductions in the Earth's ozone layer make this likely to become dramatically more common in future years, even in countries some distance away from the Equator.

In any case, the sun has an ageing effect on the skin, so enjoy it but use good suntan creams and after-sun moisturizing creams, and keep out of the midday sun if possible.

REMEMBER: sunbeds do not protect against sunburn so you still need to take it carefully when out in hot sunshine, and use the appropriate sun protection factor (SPF) lotion.

FRENCH LAVENDER *(Lavandula stoechas)*

Wheatgerm oil at 10 per cent of the base oil for extra nourishment.

HERBALISM

Firstly cool the skin as for Burns (see page 105), or by applying a chilled infusion (see page 12) of either Chamomile *(Chamomilla recutita)*, Elderflower *(Sambucus nigra)* or Lavender *(Lavandula vera)* flowers. Marigold *(Calendula officinalis)* cream may be used afterwards, or else apply the blood-red oil of St John's Wort *(Hypericum perforatum)*, which

Although expensive, Rose oil is wonderful for treating dry skin.

will take away much of the burning pain very quickly – it has been used to good effect on radiation burns. Pure Aloe vera juice is another highly soothing, cooling and healing herb.

HOMEOPATHY

Apply Cantharis, for when there is an intense burning sensation, before or after blisters have formed, and Urtica urens, for sunburn with an intense and persistent stinging sensation. For milder burns, then apply Hypericum and/or Calendula cream.

NATUROPATHY

After cooling the affected areas, apply Vitamin E cream, as well as taking Vitamin E internally (up to 500 iu daily) to improve healing and stop

Young children should always have plenty of sun-protection lotion on.

scarring. Widespread sunburn may heal more quickly if additional Vitamin C is taken (up to 1,000 mg daily for a few days). Sunburn is likely to mean dehydration, so take plenty of fluids (spring water and fruit juices, but not alcohol) in the short term.

CHILDREN'S AILMENTS

In general, children and adults are treated in the same way by the natural therapies, each person's health being considered individually and treatment given accordingly, and the same approach applies to self-help measures. There is of course the matter of dosage of remedies, and these should be reduced or adapted as explained below. There are a number of illnesses that tend to occur in childhood, such as chickenpox, German measles and measles, and children are also more prone to colds, coughs, ear 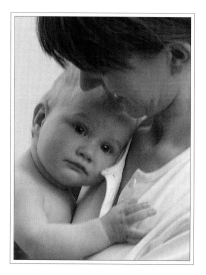 infections and the like. As well as any specific treatment for such conditions, it is worth bearing in mind some general considerations.

Children usually react quickly to any illness, showing acute symptoms that can then often subside equally quickly (much to the amazement/relief/annoyance of parents!). Due to their high levels of energy and faster metabolism, children often show signs of illness through a high temperature, and this should be looked at as part of the ailment, not as the whole problem (see Fever, pages 48-9). Because of this, it is easier for children to become dehydrated, and an essential part of treatment is to give plenty of fluids – with vomiting and/or diarrhoea in infants this can be literally life-saving. Conversely, if a child is unwell, he or she can go off food for a while, and provided fluid intake is adequate, this is not normally a major problem in the short term.

REMEMBER: Keep all medicines and essential oils out of the reach of children.

Here are some comments about each of the therapies in relation to treating children, and some of the most useful remedies.

ABOVE: Self-help treatment may not always be appropriate for children. If in any doubt, seek medical advice.

AROMATHERAPY

All the various methods of using essential oils discussed through the book – baths, inhalations, massage oils, compresses and creams – can be used for children as well as adults, with a few safety provisos.

❧ Do not use any oil undiluted on a child, except for Lavender oil on small burns or bruises.

❧ Dilute essential oils in a base oil before adding them to a bath for a child; they tend to enjoy splashing around in the bath more than adults and could get the oils in their eyes otherwise. Reduce dosage too, to a maximum of 4 drops per bath. For young infants, perhaps simply make a tea, of Lavender flowers for example, and add that to the bath.

❧ In massage, use lower dilutions of essential oils: a maximum of 1 per cent for ages 12-16; ½ per cent for ages 8-12; and ¼ per cent for ages 4-8. Under 4-year-olds will need just a drop or two in 100 ml (4 fl oz/½ cup) of base oil.

❧ Never leave a young child alone with bottles of essential oils, and always supervise their use.

❧ Use steam inhalations only briefly, and not at all if breathing is affected. Sometimes it is better to put a drop or two into a wash-basin of steaming water and sit with the young child next to it, rather than bending over a bowl.

Although aromatherapy oils may appear harmless, they are very strong and should always be kept out of the reach of children.

Eucalyptus (*Eucalyptus globulus*)

❧ A good way to help to fight infection, suitable for all ages, is to use a few drops in a plant spray, typically 600 ml (1 pt/ 2½ cups) capacity, fill with water, shake and spray the room at regular intervals. Use oils such as Lavender, Eucalyptus and Tea Tree.

Probably the two most suitable essential oils for use in childhood ailments are Chamomile and Lavender. They are both soothing, relaxing and anti-inflammatory, and help to calm the child as well as help to fight the illness. For instance, in a condition such as chickenpox, 2 drops of Lavender oil in 5 ml (1 tsp) of water can be dabbed on to the emerging spots to soothe the irritation and heal them at a much faster rate; Chamomile cream is very versatile, soothing many inflamed skin disorders. Additionally, the aroma of these oils helps to calm the child and give them a more restful sleep.

For colds and such like you may consider Benzoin, Frankincense and perhaps tiny amounts of Eucalyptus or Peppermint (also see other ailments).

Peppermint (*Mentha piperita*)

HERBALISM

Since children have a higher metabolic rate, and good underlying energy in most cases, herbs which stimulate the circulation are generally to be avoided. Herbal teas are one of the most suitable forms of treatment. With stronger preparations such as infusions and decoctions (see page 12), it is sensible to work on the principle of reaching an adult dose at age 16; hence, a child of 8 will be given half the dose, and at 4 only quarter the adult dose. This can be achieved either by reducing the amount of herb used in the preparation per given amount of water, or by reducing the amount of the preparation given to the child.

Actually preparing your own infusions can become part of the healing process.

Some of the most suitable remedies to give as teas to children are:

CATMINT *(Nepeta cataria):* for nasal congestion and catarrh, repeated colds or blocked ears; of special benefit if there is a tendency to get feverish and restless with a respiratory infection or cararrh. Both this and Peppermint *(Mentha piperita)* have a slight underlying bitterness, which indicates their usefulness too in picking up the appetite after a feverish illness.

CHAMOMILE *(Chamomilla recutita):* for most digestive upsets, from stomach pains to indigestion, the effects of over-eating, flatulence and diarrhoea. As a mild relaxant, it is a valuable remedy for calming children who get irritable and cross when they are ill, or who find it difficult to get to sleep. Do not make a tea of Chamomile too strong, in the hope of knocking the child out at night, as it can have the opposite effect at an overdose level and make them more stimulated, or irritable!

ELDERFLOWER *(Sambucus nigra):* this is the best temperature regulator in feverish illnesses; give a hot tea when the child's temperature is too high and it will induce sweating, so cooling the system. It is very helpful in feverish colds and flu, and will help to relieve catarrh as well.

LEMON BALM *(Melissa officinalis):* this is a wonderful herb for gently aiding relaxation, at the same time acting as a digestive and nervous tonic. It is very helpful in convalescence,

Picking herbs can be fun for children too.

and makes a refreshing cold drink in summer; make a tea, ideally from the fresh leaves, and after infusing for a few minutes strain and keep in the refrigerator. It will keep for 2-3 days, and a slice or two of lemon can be added for extra flavour and additional benefit.

LIME BLOSSOM *(Tilia europaea):* for tension headaches, mild digestive upsets and colds/flu with aching in the limbs. A tea of Lime Blossom at night can induce a calm and restful sleep.

PEPPERMINT *(Mentha pip-erita):* this is one of the best remedies for trapped wind, nausea and indigestion from rich or heavy foods. Another area where Peppermint is excellent is in the early stages of a cold, with fluctuating temperatures and nasal congestion.

Many of these teas may be blended together (although Chamomile and Peppermint seem to be better kept apart) for extra benefit, and can be used, suitably diluted, for infants – sometimes it is best to add 5 ml (1 tsp) to a bottle of their normal juice or water.

A posy of fresh, sweet-smelling herbs was called a tussie-mussie or nosegay in Elizabethan times and was used to ward off foul odours and potential germs.

HOMEOPATHY

Since children react in general very quickly to treatment, any homeopathic remedies can usually be given in fewer doses than might be the case with an adult. If the symptoms are less acute, or in any case for young children, try the 6c potency (see page 10) first; in more acute circumstances give the 30c potency. As soon as the symptoms are less pronounced reduce the frequency of the medication, or stop it altogether. If in any doubt about the right potency, get professional advice. Homeopathy is a wonderful system of treatment for children, with no problems of taste to overcome, and the range of remedies is very wide.

Here are some typical remedies for childhood ailments:

ACONITE: give at the earliest onset of symptoms, very good for ailments brought on by catching a chill, getting wet and so on. The child may be upset, with a hot, dry skin and a thirst for cold water, and restless at night.

ARGENT NIT: for agitation and anxiety, perhaps when anticipating some event; the child is fidgety and restless. This remedy is strongly indicated if the child has a craving for sticky, sweet foods or ice-cream, but gets an upset stomach, nausea or even vomiting after eating.

ARNICA: this is the remedy for shock, given after any minor bump or fall. It can be excellent to give before, and after, a visit to the dentist, to reduce tissue damage or bruising, and to help the healing process.

ARSEN ALB: for the child who gets fractious after any exertion, easily gets a stomach upset or mild food poisoning, and wants to be carried. Usually, the picture for indicat-

ACONITE
(*Aconitum napellus*)

CHAMOMILE (*Chamomilla recutita*)

PASQUE FLOWER
(*Pulsatilla vulgaris*)

ing this remedy is one where the child is peevish, wants to go from one person to another, and gets very thirsty, taking frequent, although small, sips of fluid.

BELLADONNA: for sudden onset of symptoms, associated with great redness of the skin and face. All symptoms tend to be violently acute, there may be over-excitability or a bad headache. This is a good remedy to give a child who has had too much sun.

CHAMOMILLA: for whining, cross and irritable children who can only be calmed with constant soothing and attention. In granule form, often at a very low potency such as 3c (that is, diluted at one part in 1,000), this makes a highly useful remedy for infants who are teething.

PULSATILLA: for mild-natured children, who are easily moved to tears, yet can be obstinate. They often fear the dark, and generally liked to be fussed over and cuddled. If the child's temperament is suited to Pulsatilla, then this remedy should be given no matter what the physical ailment.

SULPHUR: for the child who demands things quickly, and sulks if they do not come immediately. Babies get hot easily, kick off the bedclothes, demand feeding often. This is a remedy that is often used in skin conditions, such as eczema or psoriasis, and suits children with rough, scaly and itchy skin.

CAUTION
Some of the plants used in homeopathy are poisonous, for example Aconite (*Aconitum napellus*) and Belladonna (*Atropa belladonna*). Do not try to use them as herbs!

NATUROPATHY

Probably the most significant time for having a healthy diet is in the first seven years of our lives, when we are most actively developing our body, and our whole system. This is unfortunately not the easiest time to get healthy food into children. The need for energy-giving foods is high, and the metabolic rate burns calories up very fast, so snacks of fruit, fresh or dried, can be given ad lib. Intake of vegetables by children is mostly too low; encouragement and a varied diet can help, and in winter, soups and stews can be a way of disguising vegetables.

Although children love to eat sticky, chocolatey things, make sure their diet contains plenty of fresh fruit.

In acute, febrile illnesses such as chickenpox or influenza it is often helpful to allow a virtual fast for up to 48 hours (preferably check with your doctor first), but give plenty of fluids, especially fresh fruit juices. This stimulates a higher white blood cell count, improving the child's resistance to infection. Do not feed heavy stodgy foods in these illnesses; the appetite will nearly always come back with a vengeance after the acute stage has passed.

As for supplements, a multi-vitamin and mineral tablet can be useful, especially in winter. If the child is prone to colds, then Vitamin C is most important; dietary intake can be topped up with a supplement of 100 mg (1-3 times a day, depending on age and need). As girls move into puberty and menstruation starts, a multi-supplement containing a little iron can be a useful boost to the system.

The use of water applications, footbaths and so on, as described throughout the book, can be used quite effectively on children. For reducing fevers, sponge the face and/or upper body with water that is tepid, not cold, and allow to dry off naturally for a cooling effect. For dehydration, try a home-made rehydration preparation: dissolve 5 ml (1 tsp) of salt and 15 ml (1 tbsp) of sugar in 600 ml (1 pt/2½ cups) of freshly boiled water, leave to cool and keep in the refrigerator in a screw-topped bottle. Give 5 ml (1 tsp), up to 5 times a day if needed.

On the following pages are some suggestions for a few of the ailments that occur in childhood. Using the above information about the use of the natural therapies for children, and the other sections of the book, should help you treat most other common complaints. If in doubt get professional advice or treatment.

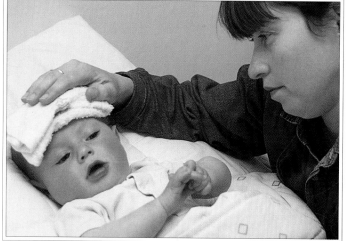

When a child is running a temperature, cool compresses can help calm and soothe the child and reduce body heat.

A well-balanced, sensible diet is the best start in life you can give to your child. Healthy eating habits, begun now, will reap rewards in later adult life.

CHICKENPOX

This is a highly infectious disease, not just restricted to childhood in fact, which is due to the same virus, herpes zoster, that gives adults shingles. It can be transmitted from an adult suffering from shingles, and in turn a child with chickenpox can give an adult shingles. The first signs may simply be a raised temperature and general feeling of malaise, and then a day later the spots appear, quickly developing into blisters containing a clear fluid. This is the most infectious stage, as the fluid contains the virus; after a few days the blisters dry up and form scabs which slowly drop off.

AROMATHERAPY

There are a few essential oils that are excellent for treating chickenpox, speeding up the drying and healing process and soothing the irritation. One of the best is Tea Tree oil. This can be made into a lotion to dab on to the spots – add 10 drops to 100 ml (4 fl oz/½ cup) water, or better still Rosewater, and shake. Since oils do not mix with water, you will need to shake before use each time. Add the oil to 50 ml (2 fl oz/¼ cup) distilled Witch Hazel for extra astringency and mix with 50 ml (2 fl oz/

LIME BLOSSOM *(Tilia europaea)*

Chamomile tea is a soothing drink for children.

¼ cup) of Rosewater. To soothe the itching skin, add 5 drops of Chamomile oil as well, or else use 10 drops of Lavender oil with the Tea Tree to give the best healing results (use fewer drops for young children, see the Aromatherapy section, page 13 and 113). Other essential oils that are effective anti-viral agents are Bergamot and Eucalyptus: use 5 drops of each as above.

HERBALISM

If the child is a bit feverish, give teas of Chamomile *(Chamomilla recutita)*, Yarrow *(Achillea millefolium)* or Lime Blossom *(Tilia europaea)* – or all 3 mixed – in 5 ml (1 tsp) doses (15 ml (1 tbsp) for over 3-year-olds) every 2 or 3 hours. Give plenty of fluids generally, and sponge with tepid water if the temperature is too high. To soothe itching on the skin, apply a little Aloe vera gel, which will also promote healing of the blisters.

COLIC

Colic in babies and infants is usually a sign of trapped wind (gas), but it is a problem that seems to affect bottle-fed babies more than breast-fed ones; this is partly due to the richness of cows' milk, and sometimes may indicate an intolerance to it. Colic, for this reason, can be noticed even in babies who are breast-fed, and may be due to the mother drinking a lot of cows' milk herself. If colicky symptoms are frequent then get advice.

Colicky symptoms can cause anxiety and sleeplessness in both the parents and the child.

HERBALISM

Where babies are breast-feeding, and having problems with wind and colicky pains, it may be easier to give herb teas to the mother which will then work through into the milk. Some of the most effective herbs are Dill (*Anethum graveolens*), Fennel (*Foeniculum vulgare*) and Aniseed (*Pimpinella anisum*); a tea may be made by lightly crushing 5 ml (1 tsp) of the seeds and pouring about 300 ml (½ pt/1¼ cups) of boiling water over them. Leave to stand for a few minutes and strain. The mother should drink a couple of cups a day. For slightly older infants, make a tea in the same way and give in 5 ml (1 tsp) doses (10 ml (2 tsp) for children over 3 years) every couple of hours until the symptoms have gone. Another useful herb is Chamomile (*Chamomilla recutita*), given in the same way.

Peppermint (*Mentha piperita*) is another traditional herbal remedy for colic, taken as a tea; this tends to counteract a number of other

DILL (*Anethum graveolens*)

homeopathic remedies, so do not mix therapies (homeopathy generally should be used on its own anyway, although there is a tradition in some countries of using combined herbal/homeopathic tablets in over-the-counter medicines). Peppermint (*Mentha piperita*) is better for slightly older children, say over 3-years-old; peppermint oil capsules are available, which dissolve lower down in the gut and so have a stronger effect on colon spasm; these should be kept for children over 8-years or so, and only used for a short time (up to 2 weeks maximum) before getting professional advice.

HOMEOPATHY

Chamomile is also a favourite homeopathic remedy for colic, given in 3c potency initially (see Homeopathy advice page 115) for infants. For children who have got colic after over-eating, or eating food that is too rich, give a dose of Nux vomica (6c potency probably will be appropriate).

FENNEL (*Foeniculum vulgare*)

HYPERACTIVITY

This is a difficult problem to identify, since the boundary between normal energetic behaviour and abnormal activity is a subjective one. There are a number of factors that may contribute towards hyperactivity, such as psychological disturbances or social pressures, and it may be the result of a brain disorder. In general, therefore, this problem needs careful assessment and qualified help.

NATUROPATHY

One factor that had been overlooked in conventional medicine for some time is that of food intolerance. Studies have indicated that food additives in particular, especially some colourings and preservatives, can trigger off hyperactivity as well as other reactions; many of these additives have been steadily removed from foods as consumers have successfully protested at their use. If your child has a high proportion of foods containing colourings etc. then it may well be worth exploring a diet without such additives to see if this makes a difference. Changes in behaviour may take 3-4 weeks to be noticeable, although strong reactions to additives can be eased within a day or so.

Children naturally seem to have boundless energy and it can be difficult to spot the first signs of hyperactivity.

MEASLES

This is one of the more serious of childhood ailments, since there are possible secondary infections that can occur. These include middle-ear infections, bronchitis or even pneumonia. These complications are often more of a problem than measles itself, so preferably get professional advice. Initial symptoms are often those of a cold and cough, although a disliking of bright lights and sunlight is quite common at the outset. A clear diagnosis of measles can be made from the appearance of small white spots on the inside of the cheeks; 2-3 days later the rash appears, spreading from the face down the body to the legs. The red spots often join together to give a blotchy appearance, and the child normally has a fever, nasty cough and feels unwell. As the rash fades, it can leave a brownish stain that disappears by itself shortly afterwards, but can linger. The child starts to feel better as the rash spreads and then fades.

AROMATHERAPY

Since the immune system is temporarily lowered (hence the possibility of secondary infections) self-help measures to enhance this can be very helpful. Constant evaporation of essential oils like Tea Tree and Eucalyptus in the child's sick room can be important; use a burner or else add 20 drops of each oil to a 600 ml (1 pt/2½ cups) plant spray full of water. Shake and spray frequently into the air.

HERBALISM

For the fever, herb teas of Elderflower (*Sambucus nigra*), Chamomile (*Chamomilla recutita*) and Lime Blossom (*Tilia europaea*) will help to induce sweating and cool the temperature; the last two herbs are additionally calming, helping to reduce the upset and aid sleep.

HOMEOPATHY

Suitable homeopathic remedies are:
BELLADONNA: for a bright red rash, sore/hot throat and overall heat, not helped by cold air or cold drinks.
EUPHRASIA: for the beginning of the ailment, with runny nose and eyes, and reaction to bright light and strong sunlight .
PULSATILLA: for itching and burning spots, causing the child to cry a lot; a dry throat and troublesome cough.

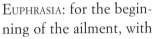

DEADLY NIGHTSHADE
(*Atropa belladonna*)

NATUROPATHY

Garlic capsules, and/or Echinacea tablets may be given as immune-stimulants. Vitamin C is valuable: give 100 mg per day for 4-8-year-olds, 300 mg per day for 8-12-year-olds, and 500-800 mg per day for over 12-year-olds, for the first week of symptoms. Half this dose may then be given until all symptoms have gone.

MUMPS

An acute viral infection, producing the typical swollen parotid (salivary) glands on either side of the jaw. It can affect one side only, in which case the other side can, although only rarely, be affected if exposed to the virus later in life. The most worrying complication for adults is a secondary swelling and inflammation of one or both testicles (*orchitis*), but this only rarely causes any long-term problems. Alongside the swelling of the parotid gland(s) there is usually a fever, symptoms settling down in a week or so.

If there is difficulty in eating, give liquids or nourishing foods. Fluid is important because of the fever too, but avoid citrus juices which may increase saliva flow and add to the pains. A cold compress can be used to reduce the swelling; a drop of Lavender oil may be used in this, or perhaps use iced Lavender tea. Vitamin C may be given to boost the immune system, and herb teas taken to control the fever and act as general tonics (see Measles for suggestions).

Homeopathic remedies to look at include Belladonna where the face is red and burning hot, and Pulsatilla for a high temperature but a feeling of chill.

NAPPY (DIAPER) RASH

An irritation of the skin around the baby's bottom when urine and/or loose bowel movements have been left in contact with the skin for too long. Small, red pimples develop, these can break open and blister, and thrush can be a complication. Try to keep the area as dry as possible, use a little talcum powder with powdered Marigold (*Calendula officinalis*) for added anti-inflammatory effect. Calendula may also be used as a cream, or Comfrey (*Symphytum officinale*) ointment may suit better. Infusions (see page 12) of Marigold or

MARIGOLD (*Calendula officinalis*)

Chamomile (*Chamomilla recutita*) may be dabbed on to the sore area and allowed to dry. Aloe vera gel can be both soothing and healing, as can a Vitamin E cream. Where the baby is breast-feeding, it is helpful for the mother to avoid strongly spiced foods, citrus juices, coffee or alcohol to reduce the irritation of the baby's urine.

SLEEPLESSNESS

Sleeplessness in children is normally due to the same reasons as in adults, i.e. over-stimulation or anxiety. There may also be pains, such as from teething, that can stop a child getting off to sleep. In the first instance, use herbal teas to act as gentle relaxants; Lime Blossom (*Tilia europaea*), Chamomile (*Chamomilla recutita*) and Hyssop (*Hyssopus*

officinalis) are good choices. Give 5 ml (1 tsp) to under 3-year-olds, a 10 ml (2 tsp) for 3-to 8-year-olds and 15 ml (1 tbsp) to over-8s, shortly before bed, with a little honey if needed. A tissue with a drop of Lavender oil on it can be tucked under the pillow to have a steady calming effect too. Look at Insomnia, for other suggestions (see page 23).

TEETHING

The pain from teething can make children very fretful, with disturbed sleep. Probably the classic remedy is Chamomile (*Chamomilla recutita*), which can be used in aromatherapy, herbal or homeopathic ways. Use one drop of Chamomile oil in 5 ml (1 tsp) of a carrier oil, and gently massage into one or both cheeks – if possible get essential oil from the Roman Chamomile (*Chamaemelum nobile*), but the

German Chamomile (*Chamomilla recutita*) is almost as good. The latter is the one used in teabags etc. and a teaspoon or two of a tea from this can help to relieve the pain and calm the infant. It can also be used in a warm compress, held over the affected cheek. Homeopathically, Chamomille will be prescribed for the typical pattern of one red cheek, one pale one, with restlessness, irritability and wanting to be carried.

TRAVEL SICKNESS

Children are more prone to travel sickness generally, and this can be accentuated if the blood sugar level drops too low, so keep a sweet handy when travelling. The best remedy is ginger (*Zingiber officinalis*), and chewing a small piece of crystallized ginger can be the simplest way to relieve the

symptoms. Peppermint (*Mentha piperita*) tea, sipped frequently, may also help; add a little ginger to it for extra benefit.

Homeopathic remedies that may be suitable include:
PETROLEUM: for when there is waterbrash and belching.
COCCULUS: when the smell of food makes the nausea worse.

IMPORTANT NOTICE

All the treatments suggested in this book are deemed safe and have been used by professional practitioners for many years. However, any treatment could cause an adverse reaction in an individual, and if this happens to you, stop the treatment immediately and seek professional advice. Do not try self-diagnosis or self-help treatment on any prolonged or serious problem without seeking medical advice or talking to a professional practitioner. Do not begin a course of self-help treatment when undergoing a prescribed course of medical treatment without seeking medical advice first.

Detailed below are important reminders regarding aromatherapy, herbalism and homeopathy treatments.

AROMATHERAPY

Essential oils should never be taken internally except under strict professional supervision. Do not increase the dosages suggested in this book. Essential oils are very powerful and doubling the number of drops is much more likely to do you harm than good.

Many essential oils should not be taken during pregnancy. Only use the doses recommended in the section on Reproduction and avoid the list of essential oils listed on page 64. All dosages recommended in this book assume a dropper that gives 20 drops to 1 ml.

HERBALISM

As with aromatherapy oils, it is important to limit yourself to the dosages suggested herein – exceeding the dosages may cause more harm than good.

If pregnant, or likely to become pregnant, only use the herbs recommended in the section on Reproduction, and seek professional advice if in any doubt. Specific herbs to be aware of are:

SAGE: Avoid therapeutic doses if pregnant, or likely to become pregnant. Sage should also be avoided by epileptics as sage contains thujone, which may trigger fits.

COLTSFOOT: Although there is no medical evidence of Coltsfoot causing liver damage in humans, some rats who have been exposed to large amounts of the herb have had liver damage. It should be taken internally only for a short period of time and preferably under professional guidance.

RESTRICTED HERBS IN AUSTRALIA AND NEW ZEALAND: The sale, supply and use of Borage, Coltsfoot and Comfrey is restricted in New Zealand and in some states of Australia.

HOMEOPATHY

Do not mix herbal or aromatherapy remedies with homeopathy – you will only confuse the treatment. It is also important to take the correct dosage as stipulated in this book. Potencies over 30c should always be checked by a professional before taking.

GLOSSARY

ACUTE CONDITION: Arising suddenly and with intense severity, but only running a short course. (See chronic condition)

ALLOPATHIC: The conventional method of combating disease by using active ingredients specifically against the disease.

ANAEMIA: A deficiency in the lack of red blood cells, or in the haemoglobin carried by them. The resultant lack of oxygen carried around the body produces a pale pallor, breathlessness and no energy.

ANALGESIC: Relieves pain.

APERIENT: A mild laxative.

ATROPHY: The shrinking or wasting away of muscles, glands or tissues due to disease or malnutrition.

BILE: A bitter green to brown alkaline fluid produced by the liver and stored in the gall bladder.

BILIOUS: Any disorder which results in the production of an excess amount of bile.

CHRONIC CONDITION: A disease or ailment that develops slowly and persists over a long period of time. (See acute condition)

DEMULCENT: Oily substance used to soften and soothe damaged surfaces such as the skin, or mucous membranes.

DILUENT: A substance used for dilution, e.g. water, base oil.

DIURETIC: Encourages urination.

DYSPEPSIA: Indigestion.

EMOLLIENT: Softens and soothes the skin.

ENDOGENOUS: Caused or produced by factors within the organism or system.

FEBRILE: Feverish, or relating to a fever.

FIBROIDS: A structure resembling or consisting of fibrous tissue.

FOMENTATION: The act of applying heat and moisture to relieve inflammation and pain.

LEUCORRHEA: White to yellowish vaginal discharge.

MUCOUS MEMBRANE: Soft tissue lining most of the cavities and tubes in the body.

PAROXYSMAL: A sudden attack or occurrence of a disease.

PERISTALSIS: Waves of contractions passing along the walls of hollow muscular organs, forcing its contents forwards.

PHARMACOPOEIA: An authoritative written guide to medicinal drugs and their uses.

PROGESTERONE: A natural hormone that prepares the uterus to receive and develop the fertilized egg.

PROPHYLACTIC: Preventing or protecting from disease.

SALICYLATES: Salts of salicylic acid.

SALICYLIC ACID: A white crystalline substance used in the manufacture of aspirin.

SUCCUSS: A special way of shaking a homeopathic remedy in order to extract its medicinal properties.

SUPPURATING: Oozing.

SYNOVIAL MEMBRANE: Soft tissues lining joints and tendon sheaths.

TRIGEMINAL NERVES: Either of the fifth pair of cranial nerves which supply the muscles of the upper and lower jawbone.

WATERBRASH: Gas being brought up into the mouth with acidic fluid.

AROMATHERAPY
Essential Oils and Some of Their Uses

Note: The uses of essential oils, herbs, homeopathic and naturopathic remedies as described in this book are listed below. These are not exclusive, nor are they their only properties, and the relevant section should always be read for fuller information on how to use them.

BENZOIN – bronchitis, coughs, laryngitis, sore throat

BERGAMOT – abscess, acne, asthma, boils, chickenpox, cold sores, cystitis, depression, menopausal problems, psoriasis, shingles, stress

BLACK PEPPER – arthritis, chilblains, cramp, poor circulation

CARAWAY – flatulence

CHAMOMILE – abscesses, acidity and heartburn, arthritis, asthma, benign enlarged prostate, boils, catarrh, chickenpox, colic, cystitis, diarrhoea, earache, eczema, fever, flatulence, hay fever, indigestion, insomnia, nausea and vomiting, neuralgia, painful periods, psoriasis, sciatica, sinusitis, sprains and strains, sunburn, teething, varicose veins

CINNAMON – colds

CLARY SAGE – anxiety, depression, insomnia, stress

CLOVE – nausea and vomiting

CYPRESS – arthritis, chilblains, fever, gout, haemorrhoids, rheumatism, urinary incontinence, varicose veins, whooping cough

EUCALYPTUS – bronchitis, catarrh, chickenpox, colds, cold sores, coughs, diarrhoea, fever, fibrositis, hay fever, influenza, shingles, sinusitis

FENNEL – colic, diarrhoea, flatulence, fluid retention, gout

FRANKINCENSE – asthma, bronchitis, coughs

GERANIUM – acne, depression, eczema, fluid retention, menopausal problems, psoriasis, stress

GINGER – arthritis, chilblains, diarrhoea, morning sickness

GRAPEFRUIT – fluid retention

JASMINE – stress, impotence, menopausal problems, psoriasis

JUNIPER – arthritis, benign enlarged prostate, chilblains, cramp, fluid retention, gout, haemorrhoids, rheumatism, varicose veins

LAVENDER – abscess, acidity and heartburn, acne, anxiety, arthritis, asthma, athlete's foot, bites and stings, boils, bronchitis, bruises, burns, catarrh, chickenpox, cold sores, colds, constipation, coughs, cramp, cuts and grazes, cystitis, diarrhoea, earache, eczema, fainting, fever, fibrositis, gall-bladder problems, gout, headache, indigestion, influenza, insomnia, migraine, muscle strain, nausea and vomiting, neuralgia, painful periods, poor circulation, psoriasis, rheumatism, sciatica, shingles, sinusitis, sore throat, sprains, stress, sunburn, thrush, whooping cough

LEMON – acne, arthritis, chickenpox, cold sores, cystitis, fluid retention, gout, influenza, nausea and vomiting, nosebleed, sore throat

MARJORAM – arthritis, chilblains, constipation, coughs, cramp, fibrositis, flatulence, gall-bladder problems, haemorrhoids, insomnia, migraine, neuralgia, painful periods, poor circulation, rheumatism, stress

MELISSA (Lemon Balm) – anxiety, eczema, hay fever, period pains and irregularity

MYRRH – athlete's foot, bronchitis, mouth ulcers, thrush

NEROLI (Orange Blossom) – depression, diarrhoea, fainting, impotence, menopausal problems, psoriasis, stress

PEPPERMINT – catarrh, colic, fainting, fever, flatulence, headache, migraine, morning sickness, nausea and vomiting, sinusitis

PETITGRAIN – fainting

PINE – benign enlarged prostate, catarrh, chilblains, fibrositis, gout, hay fever, rheumatism, sinusitis, urinary incontinence

ROSE – anxiety, eczema, irregular periods, menopausal problems, psoriasis, stress, sunburn

ROSEMARY – arthritis, bruises, chilblains, constipation, cramp, fainting, fibrositis, fluid retention, gall-bladder problems, gout, haemorrhoids, headache, neuralgia, poor circulation, rheumatism, stress

SANDALWOOD – cystitis, impotence, laryngitis, sunburn

TEA TREE – abscess, athlete's foot, bites and stings, boils, bronchitis, catarrh, chickenpox, cold sores, colds, cuts and grazes, fever, hay fever, influenza, shingles, sinusitis, thrush, whooping cough

THYME – bronchitis, coughs, laryngitis, sinusitis, sore throat

YLANG-YLANG – anxiety, impotence

WHEATGERM – sunburn

HERBALISM
Herbs and Some of Their Uses

AGRIMONY – cystitis, diarrhoea, laryngitis, sore throat

ALOE VERA – burns, chickenpox, cuts and grazes, nappy rash, sunburn

ANISEED – colic

BEARBERRY – cystitis

BETONY – stress

BONESET – fever, influenza

BORAGE – depression

BUCHU – cystitis

BURDOCK – acne, boils, eczema

CALENDULA CREAM – cuts and grazes, nappy (diaper) rash

CARAWAY – colic

CATMINT – blocked ears, catarrh, colic, fever, flatulence, influenza, sinusitis

CAYENNE – bronchitis, chilblains, colds, influenza, poor circulation

CELERY SEED – arthritis, cystitis, gout

CHAMOMILE – abscess, acidity and heartburn, anxiety, asthma, bites and stings, burns, catarrh, chickenpox, colic, cystitis, diarrhoea, earache, flatulence, fluid retention, gall-bladder problems, hay fever, headache, indigestion, insomnia, menopausal problems, migraine, morning sickness, nappy (diaper) rash, nausea and vomiting, painful periods, pre-menstrual symptoms, psoriasis, sciatica, sunburn, teething, whooping cough

CHASTE TREE – menopausal problems, pre-menstrual symptoms

CHICKWEED – eczema, insect stings

CINNAMON – colds, fever, influenza

CLEAVERS – boils, eczema, fluid retention, psoriasis

COLTSFOOT – coughs, whooping cough

COMFREY – bruises, cuts and grazes, eczema, nappy (diaper) rash, sprains and strains

CONE FLOWER – acne, athlete's foot, boils, mouth ulcers, thrush

COUCH GRASS – fluid retention

COWSLIP – insomnia

CRAMP BARK – cramp, painful periods, sciatica

DAMIANA – impotence

DANDELION LEAF – fluid retention, rheumatism

DANDELION ROOT – acne, boils, constipation, eczema, gall-bladder problems, psoriasis, rheumatism

DEAD NETTLE – eczema, psoriasis

DEVIL'S CLAW – gout

DILL – colic, flatulence

ELDERFLOWER – acne, bites and stings, catarrh, colds, fever, influenza, poor circulation, sinusitis, sunburn

EUCALYPTUS – catarrh

EVENING PRIMROSE – eczema, pre-menstrual symptoms

EYEBRIGHT – asthma, hay fever

FENNEL – colic, flatulence, fluid retention

FEVERFEW – arthritis, migraine

GARLIC – athlete's foot, boils, bronchitis, cystitis, diarrhoea, earache, influenza, poor circulation, sinusitis, thrush, whooping cough

GENTIAN – depression

GINGER – arthritis, bronchitis, chilblains, colds, colic, cramp, fever, flatulence, influenza, migraine, morning sickness, nausea and vomiting, poor circulation, rheumatism, travel sickness

GINSENG – impotence

GOLDEN ROD – catarrh

GOLDEN SEAL – sinusitis

GROUND IVY – hay fever

HEARTSEASE – eczema

HOPS – insomnia

HORSE CHESTNUT – haemorrhoids, varicose veins

HORSETAIL – benign enlarged prostate, urinary incontinence

HYSSOP – bronchitis, catarrh, coughs, fever, insomnia

LADY'S MANTLE – heavy periods, vaginal discharge

LAVENDER – acne, asthma, bites and stings, boils, burns, cold sores, fainting, neuralgia, psoriasis, sciatica, shingles, stress, sunburn, whooping cough

LEMON BALM – acidity and heartburn, anxiety, bites and stings, flatulence, indigestion, insomnia, nausea and vomiting, painful periods, pre-menstrual symptoms, psoriasis, stress

LIME BLOSSOM – anxiety, chickenpox, fever, headache, insomnia, menopausal problems, neuralgia, poor circulation, psoriasis, shingles, stress, varicose veins

LINSEED – constipation

LIQUORICE – constipation

MARIGOLD: acne, athlete's foot, bites and stings, burns, cold sores, cuts and grazes, eczema, mouth ulcers, nappy (diaper) rash, psoriasis, sprains and strains, thrush, varicose veins

MARSHMALLOW – abscess, boils, bronchitis, coughs, cystitis, laryngitis, sore throat, sunburn

MEADOWSWEET – acidity and heartburn, arthritis, cystitis, diarrhoea, fluid retention, fibrositis,

HERBALISM
Continued...

gout, indigestion, rheumatism
MYRRH – sore throat, mouth ulcers, athlete's foot, cold sores, insect bites, cuts and grazes
NETTLE TEA – anaemia
OATS – psoriasis, stress
OATSTRAW – depression, impotence, shingles
PARSLEY – arthritis
PASSIONFLOWER – insomnia
PEPPERMINT – catarrh, colds, colic, fainting, fever, flatulence, headache, indigestion, morning sickness, nausea and vomiting, travel sickness
PILEMINT – haemorrhoids
PLANTAIN – bites and stings
RASPBERRY LEAF – laryngitis
RED CLOVER – acne, bites and stings, boils, eczema, psoriasis
RESCUE REMEDY – fainting
RIBWORT – diarrhoea, hay fever
ROSEMARY – depression, headache, impotence, migraine, neuralgia, shingles, stress
SAGE – laryngitis, menopausal problems, mouth ulcers, sore throat
ST JOHN'S WORT – cold sores, insect bites, neuralgia, sunburn, urinary incontinence

SAW PALMETTO – benign enlarged prostate and low testosterone level
SKULLCAP – anxiety
SLIPPERY ELM – abscess, acidity and heartburn, boils, indigestion
THYME – bronchitis, coughs, diarrhoea, laryngitis, mouth ulcers, sore throat, whooping cough
VALERIAN – anxiety, period pains, stress
VERVAIN – depression, neuralgia, stress
WHITE DEADNETTLE – anaemia, benign enlarged prostate, gout, heavy periods, poor circulation, rheumatism, vaginal discharge
WHITE HOREHOUND – bronchitis, coughs, whooping cough
WILD INDIGO – cold sores
WILLOW BARK – fibrositis, gout
WITCH HAZEL – acne, bruises, cold sores, cuts and grazes, haemorrhoids, nosebleed, varicose veins
YARROW – chickenpox, chilblains, colds, cuts and grazes, fever, fluid retention, heavy periods, nosebleed, poor circulation, vaginal discharge
YELLOW DOCK – bites and stings, boils, eczema, psoriasis

HOMEOPATHY
Continued...

GRAPHITES – eczema, psoriasis
HAMAMELIS – haemorrhoids, nosebleed, varicose veins
HEPAR SULPH – abscess, acne, athlete's foot, boils, earache, sinusitis
HYDRASTIS – catarrh
HYPERICUM – abscess, bruises, cuts and grazes, sunburn
IGNATIA – depression, fainting, sciatica, stress
IPECACUANHA – asthma, bronchitis, coughs, morning sickness, nausea
KALI BICH – catarrh, migraine, sore throat
KALI PHOS – depression, impotence, indigestion, pre-menstrual symptoms
LYCOPODIUM – acidity and heartburn, indigestion, pre-menstrual symptoms
MAGNESIA PHOSPHORICA – colic
MERC SOL – athlete's foot, mouth ulcers, sore throat, thrush
MIXED POLLENS – hay fever
NAT SULPH – mouth ulcers
NATRUM MURIATICUM – colds, cold sores, irregular periods, migraine, sinusitis, thrush
NUX VOMICA – acidity, colic, constipation, diarrhoea, fainting, flatulence, gall-bladder problems, headache, indigestion,

influenza, insomnia, morning sickness, nausea and vomiting, cramps
PETROLEUM – chilblains
PHOSPHORUS – bronchitis, coughs, laryngitis, nosebleed
PULSATILLA – arthritis, catarrh, cystitis, depression, diarrhoea, earache, fainting, flatulence, headache, menopausal hot flushes, painful periods, prostate problems, urinary incontinence, varicose veins
RHUS TOX – arthritis, bruises, cold sores, eczema, fibrositis, gout, rheumatism, sciatica, shingles, sprains and strains
SECALE – poor circulation
RUTA GRAV – bruises, rheumatism, sprains and strains
SEPIA – impotence, menopausal hot flushes, morning sickness
SILICA – abscess, acne, athlete's foot, boils, migraine, sinusitis
STAPHYSAGRIA – cystitis
SULPHUR – athlete's foot, constipation, eczema, haemorrhoids, insomnia, psoriasis, thrush
URTICA URENS – burns, rashes, sunburn

HOMEOPATHY
Remedies and Some of Their Uses

ACONITE – anxiety, asthma, bronchitis, colds, coughs, fainting, fever, insomnia, laryngitis, stress, suppressed menstruation
ACTAEA RAC – neuralgia, rheumatism
AESCULUS – haemorrhoids
AGARICUS – chilblains
ALLIUM CEPA – hay fever
APIS MEL – bites and stings, prostate problems, shingles, sore throat
ARGENTICUM NITRICUM – anxiety, impotence, indigestion, urinary incontinence
ARNICA – bruises, burns, cuts and grazes, fainting, gout, rheumatism, shock, sprains and strains
ARSENICUM ALBUM – anxiety, asthma, catarrh, diarrhoea, hay fever, nausea and vomiting, psoriasis, sciatica, shingles
AURUM METALLICUM – depression
BELLADONNA – boils, earache, fever, headache, neuralgia, prostate problems, urinary incontinence
BORAX – mouth ulcers
BRYONIA – arthritis, bronchitis, colic,

constipation, coughs, gall-bladder problems, headache, influenza, rheumatism
CALCAREA CARBONICA – chilblains, pre-menstrual symptoms
CALC SULPH – acne
CALENDULA – abscess, athlete's foot, bruises, cuts and grazes, sunburn
CANDIDA – thrush
CANTHARIS – burns, cystitis, sunburn
CARBO VEG – acidity and heartburn, fainting, flatulence, poor circulation, varicose veins
CAUSTICUM – laryngitis
CHAMOMILLA – colic, flatulence, stress, teething
COCCULUS – travel sickness
COFFEA – insomnia
COLCHICUM – cramp
CUPRUM MET – cramp
DROSERA – whooping cough
EUPATORIUM PERFOLIATUM – fever
EUPHRASIA – hay fever
FERRUM PHOS – fever, nosebleed
GELSEMIUM – anxiety, colds, influenza, neuralgia, writer's cramp

NATUROPATHY
Vitamins, Minerals and Some of Their Uses

BICARBONATE OF SODA – bee stings, cystitis
CALCIUM – anxiety, insomnia, osteoporosis
COD LIVER OIL – arthritis, rheumatism
DOLOMITE TABLETS – insomnia
EPSOM SALTS – arthritis, influenza, rheumatism
EVENING PRIMROSE OIL – acne, menstrual problems, pre-menstrual symptoms, psoriasis
FOLIC ACID – anaemia
IRON – anaemia
KAOLIN – abscess
LECITHIN – varicose veins
MAGNESIUM – insomnia, period pains, pre-menstrual symptoms
MINERAL SUPPLEMENTS – boils, depression, diarrhoea, impotence, rheumatism, stress
SALT BATHS – shingles, thrush
STARFLOWER OIL – menstrual problems
VITAMIN A – acne, colds, eczema, psoriasis

VITAMIN B COMPLEX – acne, anxiety, colds, cold sores, constipation, eczema, headache, impotence, indigestion, migraine, neuralgia, pre-menstrual symptoms, rheumatism, shingles
VITAMIN B2 – mouth ulcers
VITAMIN B6 – pre-menstrual symptoms
VITAMIN C – acne, bruises, catarrh, chilblains, cold sores, colds, earache, hay fever, impotence, influenza, laryngitis, mouth ulcers, poor circulation, sunburn, varicose veins, whooping cough
VITAMIN E – burns, chilblains, cuts and grazes, impotence, menstrual problems, mouth ulcers, nappy (diaper) rash, poor circulation, sunburn, varicose veins
VITAMIN K – bruises
Multi-VITAMIN SUPPLEMENTS – boils, depression, impotence, psoriasis, rheumatism, stress
ZINC – acne, boils, cold sores, prostate problems

USEFUL ADDRESSES

UK

AROMATHERAPY

International Society of Professional
Aromatherapists
The Hinckley and District Hospital
The Annex
Mount Road
Hinckley
Leicestershire LE10 1AG
(For information about courses, and
essential oils)

International Federation of
Aromatherapists
4 Eastmearn Road
Dulwich
London SE21 8HA
(Provides a list of professional
aromatherapists)

HERBALISM

National Institute of Medical
Herbalists
56 Longbrook Street
Exeter
Devon EX4 6AH
(Provides a list of professional
herbalists and information about
training courses)

The Herb Society
134 Buckingham Palace Road
London SW1W 9SA
(For information about herbs and
training courses)

The School of Phytotherapy/Herbal
Medicine
Buckstreep Manor
Bodle Street Green
Hailsham
East Sussex, BN27 4RJ
(For information about training
courses)

HOMEOPATHY

The Homeopathic Society
2 Powis Place
Great Ormond Street
London WC1N 3HT
(Provides a list of medically qualified
homeopaths)

The Society of Homeopaths
2 Artizan Road
Northampton NN1 4HU
(Provides a list of non-medically
qualified homeopaths)

Bach Flower Remedies
Dr. Edward Bach Centre
Mount Vernon Sotwell
Wallingford
Oxon, OX10 0PZ
(For information on Bach Flower
remedies and suppliers)

NATUROPATHY

British Naturopathic and
Osteopathic Association
6 Netherhall Gardens
London NW3 5RR
(Provides a list of practising
naturopaths)

HERBAL SUPPLIERS

Culpeper Ltd (head office)
Hadstock Road
Linton
Cambridge
CB1 6NJ

East-West Herbs Ltd.
Langston Priory Mews
Kingham,
Oxon, OC7 6UW

The Herbal Apothecary
120 High Street
Syston
Leics, IE7 8GC

*Filling a
herb pillow*

ESSENTIAL OIL SUPPLIERS

Hartwood Aromatics
Hartwood House
12 Station Road
Hatton
Warwicks, CV35 7LG

Shirley Price Aromatherapy
Wesley House
Stockwell Road
Hinckley
Leics, LE10 1RD

SUPPLIERS OF HOMEOPATHIC REMEDIES

Most chemists and health food shops
will stock a limited supply of
homeopathic remedies. The list
below will stock a complete range.

Buxton and Grant
176 Whiteladies Road
Bristol, BS8 2XU

Freeman's Pharmacy
7 Eaglesham Road
Clarkston,
Glasgow, G76 7BU

Goulds the Chemist
14 Crowndale Road
London, NW1 1TT

Helios Pharmacy
97 Camden Road
Tunbridge Wells
Kent TN1 2QR

US

ASSOCIATIONS

American Association of
Naturopathic Physicians (AANP)
2366 Eastlake Avenue
Suite 322
Seattle, WA 98102

American Holistic Medical
Association (AHMA)
4101 Lake Boone Trail
Suite 201
Raleigh, NC 27607

American Botanical Council (ABC)
P.O. Box 201660
Austin, TX 78720

College of Maharishi Ayur-Veda
Health Center
P.O. Box 282
Fairfield, IA 52556

American Chiropractic Association
(ACA)
1701 Clarendon Blvd.
Arlington, VA 22209

American Osteopathic Association
(AOA)
142 East Ontario St.
Chicago, IL 60611

NEWSLETTERS

Alternatives
Mountain Home Publishing
(210) 367-4492. By David W.
Williams, a chiropractor

Naturally Well
Phillips Publishing Inc.
(301) 424-3700. By Marcus Laux,
M.D., a homeopathic specialist.

*Alternative Medicine: The
Definitive Guide and Alternative
Medicine Yellow Pages.* Compiled
by The Burton Goldberg Group,
Future Medicine Publishing, 1994

COUCH GRASS
(Agropyron repens)

OUTLETS FOR HERB SEEDS AND PLANTS

Cameron Park Botanicals
Highway 64 East
Raleigh, NC 27610

Caprilands Herb Farm
Silver Street
North Coventry, CT 06238

Seeds Blum
Idaho City State
Boise, ID 83706

Richter's Herb Catalog
Goodwood
Ontario
Canada, LOC 1AO

Fresh herb tea

BIBLIOGRAPHY

Davis, Patricia. *Aromatherapy, An A-Z,* C.W. Daniel, Saffron Walden, England, 1988

Editors of the Prevention Magazine Health Books, *The Doctor's Book of Home Remedies,* Bantam, New York, USA, 1991

Evans, Mark. *A Guide to Herbal Remedies,* C.W. Daniel, Saffron Walden, England, 1990

Hanssen, Maurice. *E For Additives,* Thorsons, London, England, 1990

Kusick, James. *A Treasury of Natural First Aid Remedies From A-Z,* Reward Books, Prentice Hall Inc., New York, USA, 1995

McVica, Jekka. *Jekka's Complete Herb Book,* Kyle Cathie, London, England, 1994

Maxwell-Hudson. Clare, *Aromatherapy Massage Book,* Dorling Kindersley, London, England, 1995

Mervyn, Leonard. *The Complete Guide to Vitamins and Minerals,* Thorsons, London, England, 1990

Mills, Simon (ed). *Alternative in Healing,* MacMillan, London, England, 1988

Newman Turner, Roger. *Naturopathic Medicine,* Thorsons, London, England, 1989

Ody, Penelope. *The Herb Society's Complete Medicinal Herbal,* Dorling Kindersley, London, England, 1993

Shepherd, Dr Dorothy. *Magic of the Minimum Dose.* C.W. Daniel, Saffron Walden, England 1990

Tisserand, Robert. *The Art of Aromatherapy,* C.W. Daniel, Saffron Walden, England, 1977

van Straten, Michael. *The Complete Natural Health Consultant,* Ebury Press, London, England, 1987

various. *Homeopathy, The Family Handbook,* Unwin, London, England, 1987

ESSENTIAL OILS SUPPLIERS
Bonny Doon Farm
600 Marin Road
Santa Cruz, CA 95060

Kiehl's
109 Third Avenue
New York, NY 10003

Lorann Oils
4518 Aurelius Road
P.O. Box 22009
Lansing, MI 48909-2009

AUSTRALIA
AROMATHERAPY
International Federation of
Aromatherapists
National Information Line: 190 2240
125
(the IFA has a P.O. box number in
each mainland capital city)

HERBALISM
National Herbalist Association
P.O. Box 61
Broadway, NSW 2066

HOMEOPATHY
Australian Institute of Homeopathy
P.O. Box 122
Roseville, NSW 2069

Pharmacists and outlets for
alternative remedies mentioned in the
book.

Blackmores Ltd
23 Roseberry Street
Balgowlah, NSW 2093

Newton's Pharmacy
119 York Street
Sydney, NSW 2000

Manuka Pharmacy
Manuka Arcade
Manuka, ACT 2603

BORAGE *(Borago officinalis)*

Martin and Pleasance
135 Swan Street
Richmond, Vic 3000

Bach Flower Shop
309 Little Collins Street
Melbourne, Vic 3000

Ahimsa
Drivers Court
Samsonvale, Sql 4520
(manufacturers of essential oils)

Brauer Biotherapies Pty Ltd
1 Para Road
Tanunda, SA 5352
(manufacturers of homeopathic
remedies)

Fitch's Pharmacy
731 Hay Street
Perth, WA 9000

AUSTRALIAN ACKNOWLEDGEMENTS

The Publishers would like to thank the following individuals for their contribution to this book.
Ms Penny Neuendorf, Publicity Officer, International Federation of Aromatherapists
Ms Fiona Fanner (teacher of aromatherapy in pregnancy
The Whitehouse Medical Centre, 89b Cowles Road, Mosman, 2088
Ms Robyn Kirby, President, Australian Institute of Homeopathy
Mr Raymond Khoury, Head of the Herbal Medicine Department, Australian Traditional Medicine Society.

AUTHOR'S ACKNOWLEDGEMENTS

The author would like to thank his children, Clare and Richard, for patiently posing for photographs; and Helen Sudell for plenty of encouragement, support and bullying to get the work written on time.

PUBLISHERS ACKNOWLEDGEMENTS

The Publisher's would like to thank Jekka McVica for supplying herbs for photography.

Jekka McVica at
Jekka's Herb Farm, Rose Cottage, Shellards, Aleveston, Bristol BS12 2SY
Tel: 01454 418878
(mail-order suppliers of herbs)

PHOTOGRAPHY CREDITS
The majority of photographs taken in this book were by Lucy Mason.
The publishers would also like to credit the following photographers: Deni Bown (p38, 44, 61, 67, 73, 101, 103, 105); Liz Edison (p94, 119); Michelle Garrett (p 44, 113); John Glover (p 84, 89 and 113); Angela Hampton (p116); Don Last (22, 24, 29, 32); Reflections, Jo Browne (p118), Jennie Woodcock (p 116 and 117); Zefa Norman (p110 and 111). Harry Smith (p 38, 61).

INDEX

ACONITE (*Aconitum napellus*)

PASSION FLOWER

(Passiflora incarnata)